# TEAMWORK
## for
# CUSTOMERS

# Dean Tjosvold

# TEAMWORK for CUSTOMERS

## Building Organizations That Take Pride in Serving

 Jossey-Bass Publishers
San Francisco

For sales outside the United States, contact Maxwell Macmillan
International Publishing Group, 866 Third Avenue, New York,
New York 10022.

Manufactured in the United States of America

The paper used in this book is acid-free and meets the
State of California requirements for recycled paper
(50 percent recycled waste, including 10 percent
postconsumer waste), which are the strictest guidelines
for recycled paper currently in use in the United States.

**Library of Congress Cataloging-in-Publication Data**

Tjosvold, Dean.
   Teamwork for customers : building organizations that take pride in
serving / Dean Tjosvold.
     p.   cm. — (The Jossey-Bass management series)
   Includes bibliographical references and index.
   ISBN 1-55542-491-0
   1. Customer service—Management.  2. Work groups.  I. Title.
II. Series.
HF5415.5.T55   1993
658.8′12—dc20                             92-28015
                                             CIP

FIRST EDITION
*HB Printing*   10  9  8  7  6  5  4  3  2               *Code 9291*

The Jossey-Bass
Management Series

To David W. Johnson and Morton Deutsch
*Mentors who serve me with insight and compassion*

# CONTENTS

Preface      xi

The Author      xvii

**Part One: Facing the Service Challenge**      1

1. Serving Customers:
   From Isolated Heroes to Spirited Teams      3

2. Confronting Reality:
   Discrepancies Between Good Service
   and Current Performance      20

**Part Two: Planning and Uniting**      37

3. Taking Charge:
   The Power of Working as a Team      39

4. Creating a "Pull" System:
   A Shift in Organizational Focus      52

5. Building Relationships:
   Elements of the Team-Based Organization      67

**Part Three: Creating and Sustaining          83**

6.  Encouraging Teams:
    The Need for Leadership Support                    85

7.  Forming Teams:
    New Structures for Service Efforts                 96

8.  Working with Customers:
    The Bridge to Long-Term Relationships             106

**Part Four: Refining Abilities          121**

9.  Managing Conflicts: Continuous Problem
    Solving Between Customers and Teams               123

10. Managing Frustration and Anger:
    Key Skills for Effective Teamwork                 139

    Conclusion: Nurturing the
    Customer-Responsive, Team-Based Organization      153

    Appendix:
    Guidelines for Action, Pitfalls to Avoid          165

    References                                        175

    Index                                             185

# PREFACE

*We do not love people so much for the good they have done us as for the good we have done them.*

— Leo Tolstoy

Serving people is both our obligation and our privilege; it is the foundation for a humane society. In a world that delivers quality service, parents entrust their children's development and welfare to teachers and administrators, patients in hospitals confidently rely on physicians and nurses to help them recover, and consumers are assured that manufacturers develop effective, safe products. People who serve us well enhance the quality of our lives.

As professionals, our own sense of satisfaction and success depends upon the quality of service we give to others. For example, technical support personnel feel successful when other departments in the company can use technology with ease. Teachers feel successful when students are learning and growing. Leaders can only lead when they have inspired and empowered followers to get extraordinary things done. Serving others well challenges us to be sensitive people who extend ourselves; it demands that we be compassionate, skillful, convinced of the value of our intention, and willing to work with others.

For an organization, serving customers is a "moment of truth," an opportunity for the company to demonstrate its credibility and capability (Gronroos, 1990; Normann, 1984). Delivering value to customers earns the organization respect and helps ensure that customers will return. It also binds employees together in a meaningful common mission; it is the essence of a shared vision and the ultimate "bottom line."

Unfortunately, we who work in organizations have stumbled too often in our efforts to provide quality service. Companies that fail to deliver value to customers wither as customers abandon them and seek alternatives. Disenchanted employees lose their common direction and confidence.

Complaints about service are loud and clear and directed at nearly all segments of U.S. society. After ten years in Africa, Larry Pintak, former CBS News correspondent, wrote, "In places like Bujumbura in Burundi, you [might] expect airlines to be overbooked and cab drivers to get lost. But not in the U.S. Have you flown Continental lately? Or braved a New York cab? . . . 'More for less' now means more costs for less service" (Gronroos, 1990). Disillusionment with service, however, is not restricted to the United States. A cover story in the Finnish news magazine *Helsingin Sanomat* complained, "We live in a modern society where 1,300,000 Finns take care of services that don't work—at least not well. . . . For a long time now, many have wondered what this service army is doing, as many services have either totally disappeared or deteriorated" (Gronroos, 1990).

Because too many organizations fail to serve, people in the United States and other societies run the risk of fracturing human bonds of trust and unity. We are tempted to turn away from each other and seek independent solutions. We feel unwelcome in our own country and angry at those who fail us. Sadly, we seldom realize how much we rely upon each other for sustenance, communication, and health until civil strife or natural disasters make even basic services impossible. The plight of Eastern Europe and the former Soviet Union dramatizes these risks, but we in the Western world should not underestimate the dangers we face.

Studies document that quality service creates competitive

advantage and that low-quality service is a serious disadvantage. Companies that provided superior service and product quality were able to charge 9 to 10 percent more for their products, had a return on sales of 12 percent compared to 1 percent, and grew their market share by 6 percent, compared to a 2 percent decline for companies with below-average service (Brown, Gummesson, Edvardsson, & Gustavsson, 1991; Buzzell & Gale, 1987).

## Purpose of the Book

*Teamwork for Customers* shows how managers and employees in organizations can work together to serve customers well. It provides the rationale for investing in work relationships, stipulates the nature of productive teamwork, and describes how to develop teamwork throughout the company hierarchy. It shows how developing people and "bottom-line" success go together and how service within the company is needed for effective service with customers (Schneider & Bowen, 1985).

## Audience

Because serving customers well requires coordinated effort throughout the organization, *Teamwork for Customers* is for line workers as well as staff, for employees as well as managers. Executives must communicate a credible vision for teams, managers must create a supportive environment, staff personnel must develop effective systems, supervisors must lead teams, and frontline employees must deliver high-quality service. The impact of the book will be much stronger if everyone in the team or the department — even better, the whole company — discusses and decides how to apply the book's ideas and suggestions.

## Overview of the Contents

To create an organization that takes pride in serving its customers, managers and employees must accomplish four basic tasks:

1.  They must reconcile the differences between how they want
    to serve customers and the present quality of service.
2.  They must develop an organization united behind serving
    customers well.
3.  They must lay the groundwork for employees to develop
    solid relationships with customers.
4.  They must manage conflict and refine skills in order to con-
    tinuously develop and improve the organization's ability
    to serve customers.

*Teamwork for Customers* is divided into four corresponding
parts. Part One shows how an organization can face the issue
of customer service head on. Chapter One argues that lively,
spirited teamwork, rather than isolated heroism, is what drives
quality service. Chapter Two describes the ways in which open
discussions of strategy and organization issues can help managers realize the discrepancy between their intention to serve
customers well and their present performance.

Part Two presents guidelines for how managers and employees can develop an organization that is committed to the
customer. Chapter Three offers suggestions for taking charge
of problems and avoiding the pitfalls of denial or feeling over-
whelmed. Chapter Four argues that organizations should move
away from the "push" system of producing goods and services
and toward the "pull" approach, which lets customer needs and
demands become the overriding goal. Chapter Five presents a
team organization model that describes the kinds of productive
relationships people and groups within an organization need to
form in order to work together effectively.

Part Three describes how teamwork within the organization can help managers and employees reach out and serve customers. Chapter Six offers suggestions for how executives and
managers can engage employees and credibly demonstrate their
own desire to serve customers. Chapter Seven describes how
service groups become cohesive and focus on customers. Chapter
Eight describes the ways in which frontline people also need to
develop team relationships with customers.

Part Four explains why employees need to continuously

develop their abilities and sensitivities in working with customers and each other. Chapter Nine addresses the issues of problem solving and conflict management, both with customers and among employees. Chapter Ten describes how employees can cope with their own anger and with customer provocations. Finally, the Conclusion underlines the ongoing need for the customer-responsive, team-based organization to include new people and respond to market changes in order to fulfill its mission.

*Teamwork for Customers* is intended to stimulate action as well as thought. The Appendix presents a list of guidelines to follow and pitfalls to avoid when implementing the ideas prescribed in the chapters. Readers can use these guidelines and pitfalls to review and discuss the chapters and to integrate the ideas into their thinking and actions. However, these are not simple "how-to" guidelines — an understanding of team organization and customer service is needed to make plans that are appropriate and effective for you and your organization.

To provide a concrete example of how a company can move toward high-quality service and to suggest the richness of teamwork, *Teamwork for Customers* presents the fictional case of a company I call Western Security Bank. At the beginning of each chapter, from Chapter Two through the Conclusion, you will find brief vignettes, with characters and dialogue, that present the obstacles and successes that a typical company might experience. Although the case of Western Security is fictional, the scenes are based on actual people and situations I have encountered as an employee, business owner, researcher, educator, and consultant. The Western Security example is included to help readers appreciate the profound yet practical implications of building teamwork for customers.

Becoming a customer-responsive, team-based organization is not a quick fix, but it is a workable process. Western Security provides one example of how your organization might create teamwork for customers, though you may have to be more patient and courageous. Most important, you will have to create a path that is fitting and fulfilling for you, your colleagues, and your customers.

## Acknowledgments

I enjoyed writing this book for you, my reader and my customer. I am convinced that the ideas presented in the book are very useful for helping you serve your customers and for developing an effective organization that you and your colleagues can take pride in. I hope that the ideas are presented in such a way that you can see their value. If you do apply these ideas, then I will be satisfied that I have accomplished my mission and served you well.

There have been many, many people who have served me and helped me write this book. David W. Johnson and Morton Deutsch have provided intellectual leadership and warm support for the more than two decades in which we have studied interdependence, relationships, and management. William F. Swanson, a friend for more than three decades, encouraged me to create new ways of presenting empirically developed ideas.

The book is built upon the work of numerous researchers in organizational psychology and marketing. I have been fortunate to work with managers who have both challenged and cultivated the ideas of teamwork and customer service. Jeremy Jarvis critiqued the writing of the manuscript and suggested improvements. Evy van de Vliert and Evert van de Vliert gave me a warm Dutch home in which to complete the book. Jenny Tjosvold contributed much to the writing and, with our sons and daughters, creates a family in which we take care of each other.

*Vancouver, Canada*                                   DEAN TJOSVOLD
*Groningen, The Netherlands*
*September 1992*

# THE AUTHOR

DEAN TJOSVOLD is a member of the Faculty of Business Administration at Simon Fraser University in Burnaby, British Columbia. He received his A.B. degree (1967) from Princeton University in history, his M.A. degree (1972) from the University of Minnesota in history, and his Ph.D. degree (1972) from the University of Minnesota in social psychology.

Tjosvold consults on team organization, conflict management, and related issues in diverse industries such as publishing, fish farming, health care, high technology, and management consultancy. He is a partner in several health care businesses in Minnesota. Tjosvold's books include *Working Together to Get Things Done: Managing for Organizational Productivity* (1986), *Leading the Team Organization: How to Create an Enduring Competitive Advantage* (1992, with M. Tjosvold), and *The Conflict-Positive Organization: Stimulate Diversity and Create Unity* (1991), a text in Addison-Wesley's Organizational Development Series. He is also author of over one hundred articles on managing conflict, cooperation and competition, decision making, power, and other management issues.

# TEAMWORK
for
## CUSTOMERS

*Part One*

# FACING
# THE
# SERVICE
# CHALLENGE

*There is perhaps nothing more conducive to success in any important
and difficult undertaking than a firm, steady, unremitting spirit.*
                                                    —Nathaniel Emmons


Despite the imperative to serve customers, many organizations have lost touch with their customers and stand aloof from them. Impersonal climates in which employees are expected to work independently undermine the coordinated effort needed to solve problems and create value for customers. This impersonality also frustrates efforts to create strong relationships with customers.

The very essentialness of serving customers can make it difficult for organizations to face up to the fact that they provide inferior service. Many organizations are distracted by repetitive crises that demand immediate action, are preoccupied with their own frictions and politics, and have developed defenses that frustrate a collective focus on improving service to customers. Spirited teamwork, in which people express their views directly and consider others' views open-mindedly, helps companies break out of their paralysis and provide optimal customer service.

1

1

# Serving Customers:
# From Isolated Heroes
# to Spirited Teams

*To be invested with dignity means to represent something more than oneself.*
— Abraham Heschel

Serving people is very human, and we respond warmly to stories of everyday caring. We smile when the flight attendant calms a child who is in transit from one parent to another. We feel good when we see a hotel employee searching the city to find a room for a stranded traveler. We praise those who take risks to rescue people trapped by fire or threatened by floods. We see ourselves as caring people whom our friends, neighbors, and colleagues can depend upon.

Much of our entertainment is based on the theme of serving. We watch news and talk shows that expose those who prey on the powerless. We cheer on movie heroes for doing what is right and protecting people from exploitation by villains. Many children's games involve playing at saving lives.

American folklore honors individual heroes who, against great odds and great villains, fight for the helpless and restore justice. Business lore tells how an entrepreneur single-handedly builds a business out of his or her own gritty determination, or how an embattled executive rescues a hapless company from the brink of bankruptcy.

3

It is understandable, then, that we tend to attribute good service to the good-heartedness of individuals and blame bad service on people's callousness and cynicism. Yet implicitly we recognize that poor service reflects a mutual shortcoming. Customers blame a company when served poorly and, rather than complain directly to the company, they typically patronize another. The courts and the people held Exxon accountable when its ship spilt oil in Prince William Sound and blamed Dow Chemical when its refinery released a deadly gas into the Bhopal community.

The failure to serve customers effectively is very often not caused by individuals' lack of interest or skill. Even when managers and employees want to serve, customers end up frustrated. It takes concerted, capable, collective work for organizations to deliver value to customers.

## Gaps and Disunity Underlying Inferior Service

Parasuraman, Berry, and Zeithaml (1991) began a research program in the early 1980s to measure and understand service quality. First they identified the critical dimensions that customers use to judge service quality. Customers prize *reliability,* or knowing they can depend upon a company to give them the right service the first time and to honor its promises. They also highly value *responsiveness,* or knowing that employees are willing and ready to provide service in a timely manner. Other important considerations include *assurance* (when employees are courteous and inspire confidence), *empathy* (when employees provide caring, individualized attention), and *tangible benefits* (when facilities, equipment, and appearance of personnel are pleasing).

These researchers found that customers saw service problems when there was a "gap" or discrepancy between the service they expected and what they actually experienced. This gap between expectation and service is itself caused by gaps within the organization. Managers are often out of touch with customers and their expectations because they do not listen to their customers or to frontline employees. Management is not committed enough to set specifications to meet consumer expectations. Frontline employees fail to deliver the service that management has specified. The organization, through advertising or sales presentations, overpromises customers so that service providers are unable to deliver. These are all gaps that lead to disappointing service.

Customers compare their expectations of an organization with their experience using such dimensions as reliability and responsiveness. To meet these expectations requires a great deal of coordination between management and workers, between service providers and marketing. Many companies have too many gaps and divisions to deliver high-quality service.

## Managing Interdependence

Serving customers reflects the basic reality of our interdependence. Customers depend upon organizations; organizations depend upon customers. Frontline employees must work together with customers as well as with each other. Effective service requires team effort throughout an organization and reaching out to customers. Quality service requires unity within a company; it requires joint work with customers.

### Choices

Although interdependence is thrust upon us, we have choices about how we experience and manage it. We can choose how we are going to live, work, and serve each other. Research indicates we have three major options:

*Independent Work.* I am alone. I should mind my own business and take pride in doing my job well. I am reluctant to get too close to others and believe that showing a desire to depend on them scares people away. I make sure I have the abilities and resources to do my job. Although I will protest when others interfere with my job and responsibilities, I let others solve company problems. I feel isolated at work and look for human involvement off the job.

*Competitive Outdoing.* You and I are pitted against each other in a struggle to win. I should strive to feel like a winner, not a loser. We have difficulty getting close to trust and depend upon each other. I work to develop my own resources to make myself more valuable than you. I create solutions I believe solve important company issues and press others to accept them. I have a strong drive to prove I am more worthy than my peers. My alternative is to give up on myself as a loser.

*Cooperative Team.* We are part of a team committed to a common cause in which we all contribute to being as effective and fulfilled as possible. We get close and depend upon each other for support, encouragement, and information. We form project teams to combine our expertise. We join task forces to explore problems and conflicts, discuss various views, and implement solutions that further mutual benefit. We feel united and loyal to our team and company.

Seeing options so sharply contrasted, most managers and employees quickly conclude that they want productive and fulfilling cooperative team relationships, a conclusion supported by a great deal of research (Johnson & Johnson, 1989a; Tjosvold, 1984a, 1986, 1991b). This book uses research to describe how cooperative team relationships between frontline employees and customers and between employees, managers, and executives are critical to serving customers.

I do not argue that independent work and competitive striving are never useful and should not be employed. They are generally most constructive, however, when they occur within a cooperative relationship. Team members do research independently so they can be more informed in their discussions and decisions. Departments compete over which ones can raise the most funds for charitable causes.

### Benefits

Service unites employees, managers, and customers in cooperative relationships. Many auto workers who are paid an hourly wage, for example, do not find it rewarding to work hard to give shareholders a fair return on their investment, but they can take pride in producing a high-quality, high-value car. Then they proudly introduce themselves at gatherings and relish the gratitude of car owners. But when their product is of poor quality, they hide their employment, suffer the criticisms of friends and acquaintances, and blame their managers. They stand divided from managers and customers.

The concept of cooperative team relationships is the central organizing principle that gives a company credibility and makes it consistently responsive to customers. These relationships provide a unifying thrust that ultimately works to improve customer service.

## Research on Teamwork and Customer Service

Five hundred studies, conducted by many types of social scientists and summarized in recent reviews (including meta-analyses), have documented the impact of cooperation, competition, and independence (Johnson & Johnson, 1989a; Johnson, Johnson, & Maruyama, 1985; Johnson, Maruyama, Johnson, Nelson, & Skon, 1981). The findings consistently indicate that it is through cooperative teamwork, much more than through competition or independence, that people communicate directly, put themselves in each other's shoes, support each other emotionally, discuss different points of view constructively, solve problems successfully, achieve at high levels, and feel confident and valued as persons.

Studies have also directly tested cooperative teamwork's contribution to customer service. The results point to the considerable value of cooperative teamwork for serving customers.

### *Coordination to Solve Customer Problems*

Contemporary managers recognize that they must stay in touch with and listen to their customers. Not only are retail stores and other consumer companies taking their customers more seriously; professional organizations, governmental agencies, and regulated companies are too. They must listen to customers who are frustrated with their service. But listening is a first step. Companies must also respond to customer complaints and concerns. The successful company is one that listens open-mindedly, acts appropriately, and uses customer problems to improve service and win more customers.

But coordinated action is needed to respond to customer problems successfully. Seldom can the employee who hears the complaint solve the problem alone. The employee who listens must communicate and get others to assist in solving the problem. Special efforts must be made in larger bureaucratic companies to coordinate employees from different departments with different outlooks.

My research assistants and I interviewed forty-three employees from a customer service division of a large telecommunication company about how they interacted with people from other departments as they dealt with customer problems. Employees with cooperative goals were able to coordinate to solve customer complaints more successfully than employees with competitive or independent goals (Tjosvold, 1988). When employees from different departments cooperated, customers were well served, the company's image was enhanced, time and materials were used efficiently, and employees felt more confident about themselves and their work relationships. Competitive and individualistic interactions wasted time and materials, damaged the company's reputation, and undermined future work.

A companion study investigated how engineers worked to identify client needs and provide them with valued products and services (Tjosvold, 1988). Engineering and other consulting companies are finding that their clients want viable, cost-effective solutions to their problems. Because clients want solutions to their problems, not simply technical expertise, it is not enough to give a client various kinds of engineering knowledge or suggest a solution that makes sense from only one standpoint. Clients want a solution that integrates the knowledge bases into a coherent approach that will work for them. To win and fulfill contracts, engineers within the firm must combine their expertise and experience. Their managers must work to develop a culture, compensation system, and set of procedures that encourage and reward teamwork across specialties.

We interviewed twenty-seven vice presidents and executives who manage the business development, finance, information systems, project management, pulp and paper, steam and power, civil, structural, and mechanical engineering, and fifteen other departments in a large engineering consulting company. Engineers with cooperative, not competitive or independent, goals won contracts and improved productivity by using their resources, information, and time wisely. They felt more competent and more confident that they would be able to work together in the future. When they worked competitively or individualistically, they lost contracts and weakened the company's reputation in the marketplace, wasted time and materials, lowered productivity, and made future productive collaboration less likely. These consequences cost the company money and hurt its bottom line (Janz & Tjosvold, 1985).

### The Salesperson's Network

Salespeople and customer contact personnel are expected to perform a number of important tasks (Jackson, 1985). They link the customer and company, find and negotiate solutions that are mutually advantageous, and ensure the company's products arrive as specified, accompanied by needed service and training. They are called upon to understand customer problems, provide expert assistance, and find solutions. Ideally, they develop relationships that sponsor customers' loyalty to the organization. But individual salespeople often cannot, by themselves, provide high-quality service. They turn to managers and specialists to help them structure specific agreements and to facilitate their effective implementation.

Because of the complexity of selling, many companies are relying on teams of salespeople to serve important customers. For example, several salespeople are expected to work together to serve a large industrial customer under the direction of a national accounts manager (Barrett, 1986). Salespeople pool their information to understand the customer's needs and the processes by which the customer makes buying decisions. Many companies have reported success with this structured team approach (Bertrand, 1987).

We interviewed thirty salespeople with an average ten

years of experience working for a large industrial supplier with a client base in lumber, pulp, and mining. We asked them about specific times they worked with others in their company to try to serve customers (Tjosvold, Meredith, & Weldwood, 1991).

Salespeople who believed their goals were cooperative, rather than competitive or independent, discussed issues thoroughly and made use of these discussions for consequences productive for themselves, the organization, and the customer. With these open dynamics and strong relationships, salespeople were motivated to serve customers. They also learned how to improve their service in the future. Cooperative interactions facilitated completion of tasks, efficiency, confidence in future collaboration, and positive feelings. Findings document the value of cooperative goals in fostering collaboration between salespeople and others in the company to serve customers.

Serving customers is not accomplished by the skill and flair of individual salespeople. To market high technology effectively, for example, service, training, engineering, and technical personnel must coordinate with each other and with salespeople (Tjosvold & Wong, 1992). Cooperative goals promote the open, lively discussions that produce integrated, creative solutions — solving problems and creating value for customers (Tjosvold, Dann, & Wong, 1992).

### Relational Marketing

In relational marketing, the customer and seller are both focused on long-term interests and commit themselves to each other. They make financial and emotional investments in each other and find it difficult and costly to find a new partner (Heide & John, 1992). General Motors, for example, has worked with Velcro and other suppliers to improve the quality and cost of parts (Krantz, 1989).

In contrast, transactional marketing is characterized by focus on a particular product rather than on long-term interests. Buying decisions are based on price and on the desire to reduce dependency on one supplier or customer. The cost-conscious shopper, for example, compares ads to find which store has the lowest price and has no loyalty that compels him or her to shop at any particular store.

Relational marketing is the wave of the future. Marketing researchers have recently emphasized the value of face-to-face communication and the personal nature of selling. Especially for services, the intangible aspects of the interaction between buyer and seller are considered critical (Albrecht & Zemke, 1985; Gronroos, 1990). Effective salespeople have been found to be expert communicators who combine knowledge of their products with a willingness to follow through and work for their customers (Crosby, Evans, & Cowles, 1990; Williams & Seminerio, 1985).

Crosby, Evans, and Cowles (1990) found that the quality of relationship the salesperson develops with the customer is highly related to opportunities for future sales, whereas an individual sale does not guarantee future opportunities. Cooperative actions, mutual disclosure, and expressions of interest in an ongoing relationship all contributed to a high-quality relational marketing relationship. Customers who believed a salesperson had invested in their relationship, seriously considered their interests, and demonstrated competence were open to opportunities for future business.

Relational marketing is likely to be effective in retaining customers, too, especially when the customer has specialized needs (Frazier, Spekman, & O'Neal, 1988; Soldow & Thomas, 1984; Spekman & Johnston, 1986). Personal treatment and assistance can be much more vital to quality service and repeat business than advertising or direct communication (Crosby, 1991).

In quality relationships salespeople are helpful before and after a sale, disclose themselves as people, and indicate they want to maintain a relationship in the future, and it is this manner of interacting that leads to repeat business (Wong & Tjosvold, in press). A recent study documents the value of cooperative teamwork for relational marketing (Tjosvold & Wong, 1991). Twenty-five salespeople of a large international airline and forty travel agents and managers in charge of corporate travel described specific interactions.

When the sales representatives and their customers believed

their goals were cooperatively related, they trusted that they could rely on each other, felt accepted, and did not try to dominate each other. They went out of their way to assist each other, give information, and explain issues. They explored their different views to solve problems and used conflicts to strengthen their relationships.

Because of their cooperation, salespeople and clients felt good about their interaction, made progress solving the problem and getting the task accomplished, worked efficiently, formed a stronger work relationship, and had confidence they could work successfully in the future. Cooperative interactions helped gain sales and enhance reputations.

In contrast to cooperative teamwork, salespeople and clients with competitive and independent goals tended to be suspicious, closed to constructive discussion of ideas and differences, and prone to trying to dominate the other; they had negative feelings, failed to make much progress on the task, worked inefficiently, weakened their relationships, and had doubts about future collaboration. They refused to listen and accommodate, lost sales, and felt disappointed and embarrassed.

Research supports the argument that relational marketing is critical because it binds customers to the company, provides useful information on the company's products and services, and leads to reliable, repeat business. Studies suggest that it is when sales representatives and customers develop strongly cooperative goals that they manage conflict, solve problems, and form positive expectations of future encounters.

## Team Organization

Team organizations appreciate the value of cooperative teamwork and put it to work to serve customers (Tjosvold, 1991b). In a team organization, people are excited about the company's vision and want to serve its customers. They are in ongoing dialogues about how they can get their jobs done and make continuous improvements. They easily ask for assistance and feel free to speak their minds. They respect and appreciate each other as persons and as contributors; they also directly challenge each other's ideas and positions. They want everyone, not just those in top positions, to feel powerful, valuable, and included. They forgive slights, misunderstandings, and opposition.

They realize their various perspectives and training are needed if the company is going to flourish. Confronted with complex problems and customer demands, they form task forces of diverse people that open-mindedly listen to opposing views and hammer out recommendations that make sense from a number of perspectives. They relish the give-and-take of discussing issues. They work to make their solutions high-quality ones that deserve their internal commitment. They take pride in and celebrate their individual and collective achievements.

In the team organization, managers and employees are committed to their vision. People understand how their own efforts contribute to goals of their department and to serving customers. They believe that this vision unites them. They and their bosses and co-workers have cooperative goals so that they can be successful together. They feel powerful and confident they have the technical skills and interpersonal abilities to combine their resources to accomplish tasks and serve customers well. They explore problems by exchanging information and discussing opposing views openly to dig into issues and create solutions. They reflect on their experiences to celebrate progress and learn from conflicts and mistakes.

Teamwork is part of the company's approach to getting things done. The organization as a whole envisions, unites, empowers, explores, and reflects, as shown in Figure 1.1. Groups

**Figure 1.1. Dynamics of the Team Organization.**

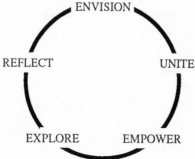

believe that they share a common vision of high-quality service with other teams and individuals. They have cooperative goals, they complement each other, and they discuss problems and strengthen their relationships with each other and with customers.

---

## Special Focus: Teamwork in Manufacturing

Manufacturing traditionally has been considered the foundation of Western economy, but more recently it has been recognized that Western countries are becoming service societies (Quinn & Paquette, 1990). The service sector accounts for 66 percent of the economy in the United States, 62 percent in Sweden, and 55 percent in Finland (Heskett, 1986). It generated forty-four million new jobs in the past thirty years in the United States, softened the impact of every recession since World War II, and fueled every economic recovery.

Until recently, managers in service industries have assumed that the key to success lies in applying the established mass production procedures of manufacturers to their organizations. They tried to standardize the product and its delivery to reduce service errors and gain economy of scale. Contemporary managers have recognized the shortcomings of this impersonal approach to delivery of services. The service "product" is very different from the goods product. Services are intangible, consumed as delivered, produced in the buyer-seller relationship, and affected by the participation of customers (Bowen, Chase, & Cummings, 1990; Gronroos, 1990). Personal customer service is now considered critical for successful service organizations.

Manufacturing managers are increasingly recognizing that they, too, are in the business of serving customers and need to use procedures developed in the service industry (Quinn & Paquette, 1990). According to Sir John Harvey-Jones (1989), former chairman of ICI, successful chemical firms "have developed an ability to provide a chemical service to customers, rather than selling a product in a bag." Customers buy an automobile to meet their transportation needs, and manufacturers are successful as they serve those needs.

The teamwork imperative applies with equal force to servicing customers in manufacturing as well as services. Teamwork is necessary within a manufacturing company to develop new products, produce ones of high quality, and build long-term relationships with customers.

As Japanese automobile and other manufacturers have shown, eliminating barriers between new product and process development and shop floor production fostered innovation and improved manufacturing performance (Cusumano, 1988). Teamwork was responsible for the impressive increase in quality and decrease of costs of the Japanese automakers in the 1960s.

Getting product designers, manufacturing engineers, and shop floor managers and employees talking and working together is critical for manufacturing excellence (Chase & Garvin, 1989). Factory managers and workers became invaluable allies with new-product developers and engineers; from their manufacturing perspective, workers gave feedback on the manufacturing potential of new designs, constructed prototypes quickly, and introduced engineering changes.

Teamwork will be even more critical for the factory of tomorrow than it has been for the factory of today. In the factory of the future, shop floor managers and workers will be linked with downstream activities in support of the sales force, service technicians, and consumers. They will give their companies competitive advantages by serving customers before and after the product has been built as well as by manufacturing high-quality, specialized, cost-effective products (Chase & Garvin, 1989).

Manufacturers are already experimenting with the idea of a service factory. For example, Tektronix, a manufacturer of electronic equipment, has set up direct

communication between customers and shop floor employees. The company inserts a card in every oscilloscope
that lists the names of the workers who built it, along with
a toll-free number. Customers call with questions about
the use of their oscilloscopes, complaints about their performance, and requests for additional products. The workers meet daily with managers to discuss the phone calls
and necessary follow-up. Workers also call customers and
ask how well their products are performing.

At Hewlett-Packard's Fort Collins, Colorado, Systems
Division, which makes computers and technical work-
stations, the factory's quality control department supports
marketing. The marketing staff learns what customers want
to know and passes the information on. The quality control department collects and presents information on test
results and conditions in easy-to-understand ways, including videotapes that inform and impress customers. The
quality department also works directly with salespeople,
through training and guided tours, to better prepare them
to serve customers.

Allen-Bradley, a manufacturer of industrial automa-
tion controls, uses its Milwaukee computer-integrated
manufacturing operation to demonstrate its products.
Within twenty-four hours of the order, the factory can
produce 1,025 different electronic contractors and relays,
in lot sizes down to one, and with zero defects. Customers
can see firsthand how various levels of controls work
together and how Allen-Bradley's software products and
systems architecture can help them.

Teamwork is key to making the full-scale service factory a reality. Factory personnel must work with marketing and service personnel if they are going to understand
customer expectations, become skilled in making presentations and consulting with them, and open up their factories as showrooms. Marketing and service people gain
essential product information and capabilities by talking
to people who build and know the product the best.

Technology helps. Computerized ordering systems, expert systems to manage complex sales, computerized logs for after-sale support, computerized catalogues for replacement parts, and twenty-four-hour answering machines to take customer complaints all speed up communication and break down barriers between production and upstream and downstream activities. However, understanding the value of teamwork and knowing how to work together drive the move to tomorrow's service factory.

Manufacturing operations continue to require fewer people. However, those who remain must do much more than any robot can. They have proven themselves indispensable members of the teams that design and develop new products. They will increasingly become partners with marketing, sales, and after-sales service as their companies strive to meet comprehensive customer needs. The days of functional groups doing their own thing with a few managers trying to coerce some coordination are gone. It is ongoing, face-to-face, spirited teamwork that propels innovation, customer service, and competitive advantage in manufacturing.

---

## Applying the Team Model

Creating cooperative team relationships throughout the organization and with customers is central to becoming a company that serves its customers and deserves their business. The essence of these relationships — feeling on the same side, believing goals go together, feeling in it together — is something we immediately recognize. We know the feeling when relationships are good for us, the company, and customers.

The model of team organization that describes these relationships is relatively straightforward. The team organization model summarizes considerable research to describe the nature of constructive work relationships. It identifies what is needed for people to work together to innovate, develop themselves, and serve customers. Yet there are difficulties and challenges in applying the model.

Within an organization, people have all been educated and socialized to see the world differently. They may not know each other well and may have different cultural and national backgrounds. They belong to departments with different priorities and styles. Still, they are asked to work together. They must collaborate in project teams under intense deadline and cost-containment pressures. Sometimes employees must work with people they mistrust and dislike.

Frontline employees may have only a few minutes, sometimes just seconds, to communicate to a customer that they can be trusted. Social workers, physicians, and many other professionals have clients whose needs are great and whose destructive behaviors must be confronted. How the team organization applies depends upon the objectives, settings, and personalities of the people involved. Working with a close colleague is very different from dealing with a new customer or a troubled client.

The model empowers people to create the relationships and organizations best for them. The model provides a common understanding and direction that people must apply to fit their purposes and preferences.

Developing cooperative team relationships requires intellectual understanding, emotional sensitivity, and the willingness to take risks and experiment. Becoming a team organization is not a quick fix to be tried out until the next fad comes along. It is an ongoing journey, not a five-step process.

How can people apply the model to fit themselves and their circumstances? By using the model together. People envision a cooperative team organization that serves customers. United behind this goal, they feel confident they can work together, explore alternatives, and find the best ways to collaborate, reflect on their progress, and make plans to strengthen their organization. The model suggests the means to as well as the ends for spirited teamwork (Tjosvold & Tjosvold, 1991).

The team organization model is an elegant, powerful, research-based approach to customer service. It binds activities together and provides a central, unifying thrust that allows managers and employees to be credible and consistent. They strive to work together as a spirited, lively team and they work with customers in a similar way. Internal service within the team organization reinforces external service with customers.

2

# Confronting Reality:
# Discrepancies Between
# Good Service
# and Present Performance

Not everything that is faced can be changed but
Nothing can be changed until it is faced.

— James Baldwin

"How are we supposed to take care of our customers when we don't take care of each other?" Catherine Capozza, head of management information systems, said to the startled management team at Western Security Bank. The other managers paused to weigh Catherine's comment.

Catherine's candor surprised even herself. Later she recognized why she was frustrated. She had looked forward to the management team's two-day retreat on strategic directions because she knew the bank needed a refurbished vision. Clarence Folger, the driving force behind the bank for thirty years, had retired, and the new president, Mark Hendriks, had pledged a more open, participative management style. Such a retreat would not have happened under Clarence's rule.

But the managers had struggled throughout the retreat. They had spent yesterday listening to and debating about each other's recommendations. Peter

Kozan, head of operations, argued that the bank should strengthen its program of benchmarking to identify and adopt the best practices of the industry leaders. Norman Pruitt, the human resources manager, wanted a program to show employees that they were the bank's most important resource, offering them opportunities to own stock in the company and providing real rewards for the high performers. Catherine proposed that investments in technology could reduce internal labor costs and provide customers greater access to their accounts. These presentations were met with understanding nods and polite questions.

The next day, Steve Kaufman, the head of the marketing department, stirred the team by talking about how the bank should be more focused on customers. It was not just what he said that stirred them. Managers were getting tired of listening politely and making little progress. The managers, especially his rival, Peter, were also annoyed by Steve's impersonal, calculating style. How could such a cold person tell them that they needed to respect customers more?

That was not, however, the question they asked Steve. Peter argued that offering a whole range of new products to focus the bank on customers was impractical given its resource restraints. Norman doubted that there would be any substantial return even if they could show customers the bank cared. It was at this point that Catherine had stepped in.

Mark, the new president, suspected that Steve's proposal was a rehash of Clarence's expensive foray into becoming a "full-service" bank, but he kept his frustrations in check. He did not want to act like a tyrant and close off discussion as Clarence had done so often. He worried, though. They were not making progress in developing a common direction. He was not blaming anyone in particular. He saw merit, even promise, in the proposals, but none really hit the target. And his own vision of becoming a more stable,

professionally managed bank that did all the little
things right seemed too prosaic.

Mark had grown accustomed to the rivalry between
Peter and Steve and had accepted Clarence's belief that
this friction stimulated the group. But the retreat made
it clearer to Mark that this division within the management team was a significant stumbling block to
developing a common direction.

Mark sensed that the managers were waiting for
him to respond to Catherine's comment. Such comments were not heard much during Clarence's tenure.
He would have met this one with a disbelieving shake
of the head. Mark wanted to encourage frankness and
distinguish himself from Clarence, but he was embarrassed by Catherine's emotional honesty. He let his
humor guide his response. "'Western Security Bank,
the bank that takes care of you'—that's our new slogan, if a mortuary hasn't already got it!"

Tension eased, and the managers laughed. Peter
said, "How about this? 'At Western Security Bank, we
take care of ourselves.'"

Norman added, "Perhaps we could have the slogan,
'After our customers have taken it, we take care of
ourselves.'" More laughter.

"I've got it. 'After we have taken our customers, we
take care of ourselves,'" Catherine joined in the fun.

Even Steve began laughing a little, but quickly
reminded the managers, "If the customers don't come,
then we can all close up shop and go home."

"There's a logic there," Norman said.

"A sobering logic," Catherine said.

Market surveys documented what the management
team had suspected: Western Security customers were
not as loyal as they once had been. The bank would
gain some new customers and lose others. They had
actually lost more customers than they had gained in
three of the last four years. These surveys also suggested that, since its association with National Com-

merce Bank, Western Security's image had become
diluted. Customers did not really know if it was still a
community bank or a branch of a regional one.

"Isn't a focus on taking care of our customers a
little general to be a strategic direction?" Peter said
with obvious sarcasm.

"But we need something general for all of us to rally
around," Mark said. "We need a common approach."

Peter did not want to lose a round to Steve. In the
past he would have felt compelled to hold back his
counterattack until he knew what was on Clarence's
mind. Since Mark had taken over, he felt less con-
strained. "I don't want to spend all our money and
effort on becoming a 'full-service' bank that tries to
provide everything for everyone. That was an expensive, exhausting, deflating adventure."

"As I understand it, the bank didn't really have a
carefully planned and professionally implemented program to be 'full-service,'" countered Steve. He wanted
to remind everyone that he had not been in charge of
the marketing department when that effort was made.

Mark nodded but thought to himself, "We don't
need this. Sparring between these guys gets in our way."

Steve, Peter, and the others recalled the many initiatives that Western Security Bank had undertaken in
the last decade. Clarence would get excited about an
issue—quality circles, empowering—and pursue it with
a passion. Then he would get disillusioned and abandon efforts until a new slogan hit his fancy. One thing
the managers could agree upon was to blame Clarence.

Mark saw an opportunity to exercise leadership.
"We're in danger of taking a fragmented approach, like
Clarence did. We have all talked about this idea or
that idea, but the issue, as I see it, is how we are
going to find a common vision and direction that we
can all support. Perhaps serving customers can be that
uniting force."

"It's basic, and I like that," Catherine said. "We

need to flesh it out more, of course. We have to define
who customers are, specifically, and decide how we're
going to serve them."

As the discussion continued they began to agree that
serving customers could be a uniting vision, bringing
focus to various activities. But they also realized it was
just a beginning point, and they would need additional
meetings to give the idea body and soul. They wanted
a strong foundation upon which to develop an integrated approach. The bank had already adopted too
many nice-sounding slogans that didn't ring true.

"I think we need to see where we are before we
begin to act," Catherine said. "What do our customers
think of us? How good are we at serving customers?
What are our strengths and weaknesses?"

"You mean, you would have us come face-to-face
with reality?" Peter said with a laugh.

"If facing reality isn't the first rule of managing, it's
close," Catherine said.

Mark liked the idea. "Doing this 'serving customers'
audit would seem to me to require Steve's expertise
in marketing and Norman's in attitude surveys. Could
the two of you work together and present results to
us in a couple of months?"

The managers considered this a sensible way to
proceed. They were glad they could arrive at even
such general conclusions with direction for action.

They spent the rest of the retreat brainstorming
ways the bank could serve its customers better. It was
fun conjecturing and probing, knowing that they did
not have to be responsible and make decisions. They
pledged to read about serving customers in preparation
for a short retreat in six weeks.

The excitement of the retreat gave way in a few
weeks to a business-as-usual atmosphere and then to a
sober, almost dejected state. The "customer audit"
report by Steve and Norman hit hard. Customers
chose Western Security because of convenience and

tradition, not because the bank offered anything superior. Quotes from customer interviews were more troubling. Customers said they did not know "what the bank stands for" or "where the bank is headed." They said the bank "is divided, one side doesn't know what the other side is doing."

The most disturbing feedback came from employees. In confidential interviews, employees complained that the bank was run by top management for top management, not for employees or customers. "It is a close race," one employee was quoted, "whether employees or customers are on the bottom rung, the last people thought about in the bank." Another said, "Don't tell me that managers are going to club us with the idea we should serve customers better." Another comment was "There's no feeling between employees and customers: they don't know us and we don't know them."

Mark briefed the managers when he distributed the report. He said they should take it as a starting point for the next meeting on strategic directions. He wanted them to use the report to make improvements and hoped they would not feel obligated to defend themselves from criticisms. He hoped, but did not want to say it, that the managers would hold Clarence accountable for the bank's present state and trust that, with new leadership, change was possible.

As the second retreat began, Mark reiterated his suggestion that the survey results should be used for improvement. The managers nodded in agreement but could not stick to treating the document as "constuctive feedback and criticism." They were hurt and angry.

Someone asked whether Steve and Norman had lost control of the report. Norman explained, "We had identified the general issues and procedures, but asked a university researcher and her undergraduate students to develop the specific ways of collecting the data and doing the interviews. We asked for an honest report, and they took us at our word."

"Can undergraduates really do interviews with employees?" Peter challenged. "Do our people take them seriously?"

"We got no feedback that the students were irresponsible or incompetent," Steve said. "On the contrary, people seemed to enjoy being interviewed."

"There will always be some employees who are just paranoid about power and leadership," Norman said. "Some people will only be satisfied if we give them everything. You can't please everyone."

"And that includes customers," said Peter. "North American customers are spoiled. They're used to fast food, fast money, everything right at their fingertips right now. When they have to wait in line for a teller to get an approval, they act as if they've been denied a fundamental human right."

The management team continued to discuss the report and its limitations. Mark grew pensive and impatient.

Then Catherine broke in. "I was as shocked and upset by some of the comments in the report as the rest of you, but we're not making good use of them. The issue is, as Mark said, how we can use this report to give us a common direction and strengthen our organization. We're blaming the messenger, here, not listening to the message."

"Let's not take all the fun out of things, Catherine," Peter teased. "I was about to talk about how poorly run that university is that this report came from."

The managers were not quite ready to consider the report's findings directly. "If this serving customers concept is so general, and we know we can't please them all, then why are we focusing in on it?" Norman asked. "I thought we had lots of good ideas about how to improve the company at the last retreat. This serving customers issue may just distract us."

"It is nebulous," Peter agreed.

"Didn't we say that things like benchmarking the best practices, reducing costs, and acquiring new technology may all be worthwhile, but that the measure of our success is ultimately whether we gain customers who keep us alive and flourishing?" Catherine said.

"What I see," Mark said, "is that serving customers gives us something to shoot for together. As Catherine said, focusing on customers puts us in a good position to decide what activities and investments will pay off."

"I hope this focus on serving customers does not mean a repeat of our 'full-service' efforts," Peter said.

"It doesn't," Mark said. "We may decide that we can best serve our customers in a low-cost way."

"Could we decide that we want to be a medium-cost, medium-service type bank?" Steve asked.

"We may decide that being 'stuck in the middle' is the best place for us," Catherine said.

"But whatever we do, we do it so our customers find real value," Mark said.

"And we should make sure that the customer finds the way we do it satisfying and rewarding," Steve said.

"And our employees do, too," Catherine said.

"What really hit me were some of the employee comments," Mark said. "I took them personally, that somehow I . . . the whole bank has failed to deliver."

"They made me angry," Peter said. "Some employees are so ungrateful; they don't appreciate what they've got. They should try unemployment if they want to feel unhappy."

"But they're frustrated for the same reasons we are. They're not serving customers as well as they'd like to," said Steve. As a newcomer, it was easier for him to accept employee criticism of the bank's management.

"Right. The good news is that unhappy employees want to serve customers," Catherine said. "Employees are already motivated. All we have to do is give them a way to channel their motivation to improve the company."

"So I should be happy that employees are unhappy," Peter said with a grin.

"We're all unhappy in that we are discontented with

how we work together and serve our customers,"
Catherine said. "That's not a problem, that's the beginning of a solution."

"Okay, serving customers sounds good, but it
doesn't sound too practical," Peter said. "What are we
supposed to do?"

The management team debated how they could improve their service to customers. It was a freewheeling,
energetic discussion.

"I'm not so sure what we have decided, but I feel
good about our discussions," Mark said near the end
of the meeting.

"I feel better about our serving customers now than
when we began," Norman said.

"It is easier to tackle something as amorphous and
important as serving customers as a team than as individuals," Peter said.

"I agree," Steve said quietly.

Catherine saw Mark smile and added, "We are
making progress."

"We are," Mark agreed.

### Reflecting on Customer Service

Managers at Western Security were struggling to get focused
on serving customers. It was easiest for them to consider narrow
issues within their areas of specialization. Peter thought in terms
of benchmarking best practices, Norman in terms of compensation programs, and Catherine in terms of improved computer
hardware. These issues were straightforward and could be debated with confidence. Serving customers is such an amorphous
and general goal, it seemed difficult to wrestle with, and progress difficult to gauge. Managers were more confident of progress
when dealing with a concrete program.

Through the many starts and stops of Clarence's reign, all
had become disenchanted with implementing piecemeal changes.
They were worried that the proposed changes would lead them
nowhere.

They began to get focused on serving customers by reflecting on their present performance. Reflection was the first step in formulating a vision and becoming a team organization. To add to their own impressions, the managers commissioned surveys to systematically evaluate customer and employee opinions.

The managers at Western Security Bank could use their own and the employees' ratings of how well the organization was doing on certain dimensions to have a clearer understanding of its strengths and weaknesses. By ranking the importance of these areas, they could eventually develop a consensus about the activities likely to have the most payoff (Dale and Wooler, 1991).

Researchers have proposed approaches to collecting data and reflecting on the current level of service quality. Chase and Bowen (1991), for example, identified some major determinants of service quality. They include preparing to serve customers, coordination between back and front offices, reliability and consistency of service, effective use of technology, appropriate degree of standardization in serving customers, appeal and functionality of facilities, logic and consistency of business hours, handling of nonroutine demands and emergencies, provision of customer privacy, rationality and fairness of customer queuing, availability of materials, orientation of new customers, collection and use of customer feedback, and selection and training of employees. Using these service dimensions, Chase and Bowen constructed a questionnaire organizations such as Western Security can use to rate themselves.

## Coping with Defenses

Managers at Western Security had strong feelings about the feedback from customers and employees. The need to be respected and valued by others is very basic, and evidence of failure can provoke defensiveness and rationalization. Managers tried to protect themselves by dismissing the complaints of customers and employees. However, blaming the messenger, finding excuses, and employing other defenses do not get Western Security closer to its goal. It is ironic, and sometimes tragic, that feedback indicating ineffectiveness on important issues is often the most difficult to accept and use.

Top managers have been found to block out feedback that evokes strong feelings (Argyris, 1991; Argyris and Schön, 1978). Managers and other professionals typically want to avoid confronting evidence that they have performed ineffectively. They feel that behaving less than perfectly means failure, and, because they so often succeed, are unskilled at coping with shortcomings. Behind this defensiveness is the managers' commitment to seeing themselves as winners who can cope rationally with problems and remain in charge.

Teamwork helps managers and employees cope with the emotional demands created by reflecting on customer service problems. Team members give each other support so that they can see that the feedback is well intentioned and useful, and so that they do not exaggerate its negativity. No one person has to bear full responsibility for failures because the causes lie within the organization as a whole.

Feedback on customer service is difficult to understand and use. People are tempted to shrug off the issue as faddish or impossible to address. However, in a team people can feel they have the collective problem-solving ability and clout to make meaningful changes. They can translate their analysis into useful action.

In the early 1980s, Tom Page, executive vice president at Ford's Diversified Product Operations (DPO), whose eight divisions made automobile parts for Ford assembly plants, wanted to get all managers behind Ford's quality and teamwork vision (Jusela, Chairman, Ball, Tyson, & Dannermiller, 1987). But first how could the managers' defenses be confronted? According to them it was government policy, bad luck, and unfair competition by the Japanese that had caused the temporary downturn in revenue.

Page had large groups of Ford DPO managers listen to operators of Ford franchises and buyers of Ford cars as they revealed their personal frustrations and complaints. Ford managers also listened to Americans sing the praises of the Japanese cars they owned. This group confrontation helped convince Ford managers that they needed to improve the quality of their cars and service, and they could work as a team to do so.

Together managers can discuss the value of quality service to themselves as individuals and to the company as a whole. They can work beyond the defensive stance that the status quo is acceptable. They can see for themselves, in concrete terms, how improving service will pay off. Managers and workers, together, can also consider their common fate if customer service is not improved.

---

### Case Study: W. T. Grant's Downward Spiral

Confronting reality and reflecting on customer service can be hard, emotional work that top management continually postpones. Change is ever present, but management often fails to appreciate changes in the environment and in their organizations soon enough to take effective action.

The decline and eventual dissolution of W. T. Grant illustrate the dangers of being out of touch with customers and failing to develop teamwork to take corrective action (Weitzel & Jonsson, 1991). Founded in 1906, Grant grew into the nation's second-largest chain of variety stores; but, after a decade of decline, it was dissolved in 1976.

In the 1960s, Grant began an aggressive expansion program but lacked a system for assessing the stores' ability to serve customers and achieve profitability. The stores were so autonomous that central management was unable to oversee their policies. For example, most shoppers at Grant were women, but there was no attempt to develop a consistent image and position to serve their needs.

Years into the expansion program, top management finally faced the reality that there were serious problems. For example, they discovered that sales per square foot were less than half those of the company's competitors. Yet top management was unable to alter its policy of expansion. Business continued as usual, even though customers were switching to discounters like K-Mart, Wal-Mart, and Target, which offered lower prices and name brands. Upscale customers were moving to J. C. Penney, Nordstrom, and other department stores.

Late in the 1960s, Grant did make some changes, though it continued with its expensive and debt-based expansion program. The program made it easier for customers to buy on credit, which increased sales, but accounts receivables ballooned. In 1974, the company wrote off $92 million for bad debts.

Grant's poor financial performance, caused by inferior customer service and bad management, eventually made it obvious that drastic change was necessary. A new CEO, James Kendrick, replaced Richard Mayer in 1974. He drastically reduced expansion, but had difficulty projecting a clear image to customers. There was little information about which items were selling or who their customers were. Suppliers were hesitant to ship for fear that Grant would enter bankruptcy and be unable to pay.

By 1975, Grant was so much indebted to banks that Kendrick was replaced by Robert Anderson, who had ambitious plans to close stores and find a new direction. Six months later, Grant went into bankruptcy. Problems were so large that in February 1976, under pressure from creditors, the stores closed forever.

Behind the blindness, inaction, faulty action, and dissolution of Grant lay the failure to develop spirited teamwork focused on the customer. Top management was out of touch with customers, store managers, and personnel who could have kept them informed about changes in the marketplace. Nor did managers fully discuss the changes and problems they knew about or brainstorm alternative plans. President Mayer and Chairman Staley insisted all decisions must be funneled through them. It was a company joke that a person became a Grant director according to how fast he could say yes. However, when problems are obvious and a crisis is reached, it can be very difficult to discuss opposing views and create effective solutions (Tjosvold, 1984b).

By the time reality penetrated the defenses of Grant's top management, problems were very severe. Without customer or supplier loyalty, and without teamwork inside the company, new management was unable to turn Grant around.

---

## Moving Toward an Integrated Approach

Western Security, like many other companies, had adopted many slogans and programs to address the competitive, turbulent marketplace and reflect the changing values of employees. They talked about "people first" and "making everyone a winner"; they wanted to be a "full-service" bank that offered a dazzling array of products; they invested substantially in technology for twenty-four-hour customer access.

These programs all made sense and were — at least in part — successful. However, the company never realized the expected returns. Clarence became disgruntled and then found a new slogan to pursue.

These programs not only failed to unite employees but actually contributed to divisiveness. Clarence would lavish attention and funds on marketing in the "full-service" phase, then on human resources in the "employees first" phase, and so on. The department heads competed for these resources. Once a particular program was instituted, other departments had no vested interest in its success. Indeed, they would wait until the program had played out, hoping for an opportunity to head the next foray.

Investments in technology, research and development, restructuring, and marketing may or may not be wise for an organization. The decision to reduce costs at the expense of quality or to improve quality and increase costs may or may not be prudent. Programs should not be undertaken because they sound contemporary and other companies are doing them, but because they help the company offer improved value to their customers. A shared vision for serving customers provides a concrete criterion for success.

## Working Together

Managers at Western Security were distracted from serving customers because of their own internal competition. For some organizations, political infighting is so entrenched and pervasive that people lose touch with the customer altogether. People are too busy fighting each other to worry about the competition and the customer (Eisenhardt, 1989; Eisenhardt & Bourgeois, 1988). Sometimes coalition-building and influencing policy become so elaborate that managers become enchanted with the subtleties and hone their skills to a fine art. The idea that they are to work together to serve customers sounds too straightforward and dull.

Fortunately, Western Security managers were not highly committed to political infighting. With the president's determination and an open discussion of the issues, they were able to come to terms with evidence of their ineffectiveness. Then they were in a position to use the data constructively.

Western Security managers were learning that to be successful they would have to be united. Serving customers well is such a challenging, complex task that no one can do it alone. As a team the managers could identify their specific strategies: who their customers were and how they were going to provide them with value. They would work together to establish an organization that would fulfill that strategy.

But how could they create that specific strategy and the organization to reach it? The management team began to discover that through direct controversial discussion of opposing views they could identify issues, explore problems in depth, and create solutions. This lively collaboration proved critical as the managers developed a meaningful, practical common direction for the company.

Spirited teamwork also characterizes the kind of organization the managers wanted to develop. Serving customers cannot be mandated by top management. It requires the commitment and persistence of employees throughout the organization. Employees must invest their hearts as well as their minds in developing and delivering value to customers. Employees have to help their company compete in the tough marketplace, but they also have to serve customers humanely, with a personal touch. Such commitment cannot be coerced or bought; disgruntled employees cannot simply be silenced.

Managers must take the lead to create an organization in which employees work well together and with managers. Managers and employees must respect each other as allies in a common cause, believe their ideas and work are appreciated, and consider their treatment fair and motivating. In this environment employees are prepared to reach out and serve customers.

To reflect on their present level of customer service, Mark and other managers at Western Security had to collect and analyze information, deal with their defenses, and develop a common approach. To assess their position and forge a common direction required a great deal of lively, spirited teamwork. Opinionated presentations and polite questions did not, by themselves, create a common ground. By exploring their views in a give-and-take discussion, they appreciated the imperative for an integrated approach to strengthening the company's customer service.

## Part Two

# PLANNING
# AND
# UNITING

*The five separate fingers are five independent units. Close them and a fist multiples strength. This is organization.*

        —J. C. Penney

*For more than 80 years we have practiced . . . our tradition of management through partnership. . . . We have found a unique way to blend our cooperative spirit with individual responsibility. At J. C. Penney we have a management tradition that has sustained us well through more than 80 years of growth. This tradition began with Mr. Penney and grows out of his concept of partnership. Through the years it has served as our unique foundation.*

        —Bill Howell, Chairman, J. C. Penney Company

Serving customers is an organization-wide responsibility; it takes collective effort to provide value to customers. The top management group needs to feel it has the power to begin to improve the organization's customer service, but it must also empower managers and employees to be valuable partners.

Contemporary managers realize that traditional notions of internal efficiency may not translate to effective delivery of service to customers. As discussed in Chapter Four, they are challenging individualistic ways of working and experimenting

with "pull organizations" where individual customer demands
"pull out" employees and resources as needed.

Pull organizations require employees to combine their expertise to serve customers. Synergy throughout an organization
fuels the innovation needed to serve customers with new products
and services in the future. The team organization model summarizes knowledge about the nature of productive teamwork
in organizations.

3

# Taking Charge:
# The Power of Working
# as a Team

*To attain happiness in another world we need only to believe something, while to secure it in this world we must do something.*
                                              *—Charlotte Perkins Gilman*

"We've survived a lot," Norman said as he entered Peter's office. "I guess we can survive Mark's 'serving customers' brainstorm."

"I'd have thought you would go for it, being a 'touchy-feely' kind of guy," Peter teased.

"It's my *budget* that's going to be touched," said Norman quickly. "I'm going to be asked to change our seletion procedures and do different kinds of training, and do it all with smoke and mirrors, not more money." Though he did not like to admit it, Norman worked hard to convince Peter that he, too, was a "bottom-line" manager. He envied Peter's ability to project that image, seemingly without much effort. Proving that you were a tough-minded manager was, he concluded, a special burden for human resource managers.

"Same here," Peter agreed. "We're going to pay, and Steve's going to get all the credit."

"We don't have to worry much — this phase will pass too." Norman had taken Peter's side in the competition with Steve. He was hoping his man would win and end up in the president's chair.

"Mark says that the 'serving customers' strategy is going to be a mutual, common direction."

"Talk's cheap. I'll believe it when I see it," said Norman.

"Maybe we should force the issue a little," Peter said. "We might just have to remind Mark that it's supposed to be a team thing where everyone contributes and everyone benefits."

Norman and Peter continued to discuss their misgivings about Mark's push for serving customers. Although they mostly repeated and rehashed, they both found their conversation satisfying. Yet they knew it would be risky for them to appear to be undermining Mark's efforts. It would be more prudent to let events unfold and wait for an opportunity to reassert themselves.

Feeling unburdened as he left Peter's office, Norman said to himself, "I'm glad I'm on Peter's side, but it bothers me that, while he seems to talk with me in confidence, he never initiates."

Mark was optimistic that the managers could find serving customers a common ground upon which to strengthen Western Security. They would create a strategy that would really unite and ignite the organization. Yet dark thoughts kept creeping across this rosy picture. Could he really expect Steve and Peter to put aside their rivalry? The managers were such strong, independent individuals — Clarence had urged them to be. How could they really become a team? Departments at Western Security had almost no experience actually working together, and Clarence had made them compete for recognition and prizes.

But Mark was a man of action more than reflection.

He thought about the eventual payoffs and what steps he needed to take. He did not dwell on the barriers and future problems.

His objective for the next strategy session was straightforward: the managers needed to identify who were the customers they would serve and how they would do it. His plan was simple: have the managers discuss and decide.

To begin the meeting, Mark stated his objective and threw it open for discussion. The managers soon faltered as they found it difficult to get a handle on what the theme of serving customers actually meant. Peter reiterated his concerns about the frustrations and costs of trying, again, to become a "full-service" bank. Norman doubted that the bank could really satisfy customers whose expectations kept rising.

Steve knew he should try to be more patient. Getting angry and barking were effective as he worked his way up the ladder, but he realized that Peter and the other managers would not tolerate being the targets of such anger. After listening to Peter and Norman for a while, Steve tried to hide his impatience and to sound like he was taking the high ground. "You're talking as if serving customers is an option, but it isn't. We must, if we want to survive. It will also give us a common goal that we can work together to achieve."

Peter was angry, which gave him energy to speak directly and clearly. But the energy was so intense he felt the words coming out before he had time to check them. "Lectures and pompous slogans are not going to get us where we need to go. The people who make this bank go are going to have to do a lot of work. We'll need new systems and procedures. The operations people will need to be encouraged, supported, and rewarded. They don't need more nice-sounding ideas to listen to."

Steve was caught off guard. He tried not to bark back, but the words came out. "We can't just keep doing our thing. The marketplace is changing, and we have to change with it."

"Are we just supposed to be leopards and keep changing our spots every time the marketplace changes, or some self-styled expert says it has changed?" Peter shot back. "Where's our credibility, our presence, our stability?"

"But where is our innovation?" Steve replied. "What good is it for us just to stay the same? We need to update and keep abreast, and understanding the needs and wants of our customers can be the foundation for that."

"Words, words . . . we need action," Peter said.

"But we need a plan," Steve said.

"Okay, we develop beautiful phrases and elaborate plans," Peter said. "So what? What difference does it make? The whole plan must be implemented, and who is going to do that?"

"All of us," Steve shot back. "We must all serve customers. It's something that we do together . . . it gets managers, employees—everyone together."

"But how do we get this great big ship of a company turned around to do it?" Peter asked rhetorically. "And once it is turned around, who's to say we will not just try to turn it back?"

"Serving customers will not go out of style," Steve countered.

The energy of the conflict was fading and Peter and Steve were reasserting their self-control. They were both still defiant, but they were also embarrassed that they had let their buttons be pushed. They were surprised by how their colleagues reacted.

"Good debate," Catherine said, nodding her head approvingly.

"Well spoken," Mark agreed. Mark had wanted to step in as the conflict first developed, but could not think of what to say. Now he was glad that he had not intervened.

"Well done on both sides. Let's have more of these debates," Norman said.

"It was fun," Peter said.

"It was?" replied Steve.

"When you win, anything is fun," Peter said.

"I think we're all winners," Catherine said.

Mark saw an opportunity to lead. "Peter and Steve helped us articulate just why we should be serious about serving customers. They also suggested some of the difficulties and barriers we face if we are to improve. Let's keep this discussion going to try to identify our major tasks."

After an hour, the managers were coming to a consensus on important points:

1.  Serving customers is a credible direction that Western Security can commit itself to for the long term. Serving customers is not going to get outdated.
2.  Serving customers well requires knowing who we are and who our customers are. We must know what they want and value, and we must know our abilities and interest in delivering these values.
3.  Serving customers provides stability and promotes innovation. We are committed to our customers and are willing to adapt to serve them better.
4.  Managers cannot impose the ability and desire to serve customers on the rest of the organization. Employee involvement and participation are necessities, not management choices.
5.  It is only through teamwork by managers and employees that we can successfully serve customers.

After a break, Norman said, "How come the five points we have agreed upon look so simple? We put in good, hard work to get them up on the board."

"Truth is usually simple, but that doesn't mean it's simple-minded," said Catherine.

"In a way we have decided a lot, and in another way we have not decided much," Mark said.

"It's important to get off on the right foot. If we're not heading in the right direction, we're not going to get where we want to go," Peter said.

"We have a journey ahead of us," said Steve.

The good feelings and sense of being on top of the issue got them quickly back into discussing future action. The excitement and energy, though, did not give rise to quick solutions. Ideas were proposed, but shortcomings and loopholes were noted. The managers' energy had not dissipated but was manifested in heated discussion and debate that at once exhilarated and frustrated them. How could they turn around a whole organization and point it in the right direction?

"I hate to sound like a coward," Catherine began with a laugh, "but I don't think we're in a position to make decisions about the next steps. Actually guiding this process of becoming a quality service company is not something we can just decide in a few hours. We need to involve the whole organization."

"How big do you want the table?" Peter asked. "Let's invite everyone in and have a shoot-out."

"Maybe we should close the bank down for a day or two," said Norman.

"I can see it now, we could put out signs that read, 'Our Valued Customers: We are closed so that we can serve you better,'" Steve said.

"Provocative ideas," Catherine mused. "Let's make sure the minutes clearly record whose they are! I was thinking along more prosaic lines, something like having a task force made up of representatives throughout the organization to consider and guide our collective efforts."

"When the going gets tough, form a committtee," Peter teased.

"Beats when the going gets tough, do something stupid," Catherine teased back.

The more they discussed the idea of a cross-sectional task force, the more they liked it. They thought the task force could potentially give them more and better ideas about how to improve service to customers. The second major advantage would be greater buy-in: people across the organization would be more likely to understand and commit to the program.

The managers debated the extent to which the task force should be autonomous. Peter argued that it is a well-recognized fact in manufacturing circles that work teams must be at least semiautonomous. Task force members would not really buy in if they were always second-guessed. They needed the autonomy to be self-directed and self-motivated.

Yet the more they discussed this idea, the more trouble they had with it. The task force was to help top management and the rest of the organization. They could not be autonomous. The task force and the managers needed dialogue and exchange, not independence.

"But surely the task force must have some autonomy," Peter said.

"I think we all agree that it needs leeway to develop ideas," Catherine said. "We don't want it figuring out what we want and giving it to us."

"But if the task force doesn't have clout, that's what will happen," Peter said.

"We can't just hand over our responsibilities and authority," Steve said. "We've got to stay in charge."

"I think we can convince the task force that they will have power and authority because we're looking for their ideas," Mark said. "We'll make it clear that we won't use them to justify unpopular decisions, and we won't simply reject what they offer. We'll pledge to consider their suggestions open-mindedly."

"Believe it or not, I agree wholeheartedly with Mark," said Peter. "I'm trying to win back some points for being so rowdy all day.

"Finally, you're getting with the program," Mark joined in.

"This whole task force idea could be fun to watch," Norman said. "We can get people talking to each other who normally don't have the opportunity."

"The give-and-take between the task force and us sets a credible direction," Catherine said. "That kind of lively debate is what we need, I think, to serve customers well."

"Our method reinforces the message," Peter clarified.

"I like it that we're assuming our employees want to improve our service to customers," Norman said. "We're not assuming that we have to push them into it. We're setting up good, positive expectations."

"Yes, we're asking our people to contribute, to help us be a company they can be proud of," Mark said. "We're not just telling them how to act, but treating them as partners. Like the five points on the board, it's a simple — but not simple-minded — idea."

### Feeling Powerful

Mark and the other managers were beginning to feel they were in charge of how to improve customer service. They had confronted the issue, reflected on feedback, and developed ways to proceed. At times they fell back into pessimism and despair, but they kept plugging away and making progress.

What was critical was that they were breaking out of their divisive ways of working. The managers had formed temporary alliances under Clarence to protect themselves. But with Mark's openness, direct discussions were encouraged between managers, and alliances became less useful. Managers were able to raise their objections openly and have them addressed and incorporated into the common direction. It is through such constructive discussion of conflicts that unity is forged (Tjosvold, 1991a).

Working together as a team is invigorating and empowering. People know that their own ideas and perspectives might be biased and limited. Even autocratic managers usually have someone they rely on as a sounding board for their ideas. Controversial discussions help people cope with their individual limitations: blind spots are identified, premature conclusions checked, and unwarranted assumptions probed (Tjosvold, 1985a, 1991a). Through give-and-take discussion, people elaborate on their ideas, break out of traditional ways of thinking, and integrate positions to create new solutions not previously considered. Especially in organizations where decisions must reflect a variety of perspectives, team problem solving is critical to moving forward.

Teams are also useful for grappling with the emotional side of solving problems and changing an organization. Change raises perplexing anxieties and intense hopes. Fears can paralyze managers and lead them to think defensively and rely on well-known but outdated solutions. Optimism and positive expectations can also interfere with progress, when managers make rosy assumptions that lead to careless solutions.

By discussing their fears and hopes, managers can put them into better perspective. They find out whether others see the same dangers; they help each other cope. When faced together, fears lose much of their sting. By checking the basis of their hopes and expectations, managers can more realistically assess the risks of new ventures and determine ways to minimize them.

Yet as Mark and the other managers at Western Security were finding out, teams must become skilled at dealing with the emotions caused by facing issues head on. Scheduling regular meetings is not enough. People must be able to express their views directly and to consider other positions open-mindedly.

Now, Western Security managers face additional challenges in encouraging the customer service task force to engage in constructive exchange. If they are successful, the task force will be able to make use of its members' diverse perspectives and expertise to discover a vital new direction for the bank.

### Power in Teamwork

Power is traditionally defined in terms of dominating others and getting them to do what one wants. We have power to the extent that others do not. To be powerful requires enhancing oneself while diminishing others. Power defined this way is a disruptive force. It corrupts people who have it and enfeebles those who do not. The best that can be achieved is for an organization to minimize impact through power equalization.

But this zero-sum, win-lose, competitive view of power is only one of its faces. Power can be a highly positive force in organizations (Kouzes & Posner, 1987). It can energize and promote productivity (Pfeffer, 1981). Powerful managers have the resources and confidence to encourage employees (Kanter, 1979).

Experiments and field studies have documented the cooperative, constructive face of power (Tjosvold, 1981, 1985b, 1985c, 1990; Tjosvold, Andrews, & Struthers, 1991, in press). Managers and employees can feel powerful as they empower each other. When they are members of a cooperative team, people support and encourage each other and provide each other with resources and assistance. Managers with power and cooperative goals use their resources to help employees be productive, whereas competitive and individualistic managers, while able, are unmotivated to help (Tjosvold, 1985b).

Feeling powerful comes from the confidence that one has the abilities and wherewithal to move forward, solve problems, and be successful. In a cooperative team, people feel more powerful because they know that they can use their team members' resources as well as their own. In contrast, when confronted alone with a complex, difficult challenge, people can be demoralized, having to rely only on their own abilities.

---

### Case Study: Empowering New York City Police

Lee P. Brown, newly appointed police commissioner of New York City, has a mission to empower police officers and the neighborhoods they serve (Webber, 1991). He and his management team have confronted the reality that traditional policing is not working. While police continue to arrest people in record numbers and fill prisons to overcrowding, members of the community do not feel safe. This fear may be more costly than being a victim of crime. Fear reduces the quality of life and the economic and social activities that hold a neighborhood together.

Brown and other police can easily point to the social problems that underlie the violence and crime New Yorkers experience. Too many families and schools fail to provide their children with direction, purpose, and skills. As many as 50 percent of the students who start school do not finish it. Of those who complete school, as many as 25 percent may be functionally illiterate and unprepared for the world of work. Drugs wreak enormous havoc and have made violence an everyday experience. However, rather than use these conditions as excuses, the New York City Police Department wants to become an agent for dealing with the causes of crime.

Under current conditions, the traditional police methods of random patrol response to emergency calls, and criminal investigation are ineffective for reducing crime and making people feel safe. Studies have repeatedly shown that random patrolling does not reduce crime or fear. Police officers spend nearly 90 percent of their time responding to emergency calls. On average, New York City police make 11,700 radio runs per day, but to no great effect. Investigations result in arrests in less than 20 percent of all robberies and 10 percent of all burglaries. The police are putting out fires, not identifying and solving problems or catching criminals in action.

Brown's vision is community policing. Here police officers become the central focus of a neighborhood. Police officers get to know people and work with them to improve the quality of life, reduce the fear of crime (brought on by noisy teenagers, littered hallways, and dark alleys), and solve the problems that cause crime. People in the neighborhood are to know their police officers by name and feel that they can trust them. Rather than blame the police for not catching criminals, they work with them to provide information and improve their neighborhood. The purpose of community policing is to reduce crime and criminal victimization, revitalize community problem solving, and restore faith that the community is a safe place.

Making the transition to effective community policing will require massive organizational change. The New York City Police Department has had an impersonal, command-and-control culture that is incompatible with trusting police officers and giving them the autonomy to work with their neighborhoods. The organization must encourage them to be sensitive people able to work with the community—not conformers who follow orders and procedures. Rather than fearing punishment for making waves, patrol officers must feel that they will be supported by top management. Rewards systems based on numbers of arrests should be changed to reward police for reducing crime and continuing patrol work. Awards should be given for improving the quality of life in neighborhoods as well as for arresting hardened criminals.

A major barrier to these changes is that New York City police officers are not used to working together as a team or working with management. Many police officers recognize the need for change but are skeptical that top management is really committed to change and has the political independence to follow through. In place of camaraderie, there are suspicion, bureaucratic layers, and fragmentation.

A great deal of spirited, cooperative teamwork will be needed to make community policing a reality. Police officers will have to discuss and create a culture and system that empower them. They must experiment together with new ways to solve problems and make neighborhoods safe. They will have to learn how to work as a team with community members so that, together, they feel empowered to deal with the tough problems of crime and fear in New York City.

## Empowering Others

The managers at Western Security first thought that they could use their power to directly determine the bank's course. They came to see that to influence the rest of the organization successfully they would have to empower others.

Managers typically think of power in zero-sum ways. If they have power, others do not. If others do, then they do not. Yet the managers at Western Security were coming to sense how limited this view was. They began to feel more influential and powerful when they confronted the bank's problems together.

Peter's argument for giving the customer service steering committee autonomy was based on the traditional idea of power as zero-sum. The steering committee would have power only to the extent that the management team did not. But strict autonomy for the task force or for other teams in an organization is a recipe for powerlessness, not power. It is only by combining forces that the task force and the management team can be powerful. They need dialogue, discussion, and debate so that they can influence each other and contribute as a group to improving customer service at Western Security.

The steering committee and management team will have to apply this learning as they work to involve the rest of the organization. The managers cannot force employees to do things that employees do not want to do. Rather the managers must empower the whole organization to do what everyone wants: to contribute to a company that deserves commitment and pride because it gives value to customers. The next chapter describes how pull organizations can improve customer service.

# 4

# Creating a
# "Pull" System:
# A Shift
# in Organizational Focus

*To improve the golden moment of opportunity and catch the good that is within our reach is the great art of life.*
*—Samuel Johnson*

"I know you expect bond paper from my office," Mark said with a smile as he passed out the list of five principles the managers had agreed would guide their drive to serve customers. "We decided that using regular copy paper was more fitting, given that we expect this list to be changed and improved."

"Yes, we worked together to come up with a symbolic and cost-effective solution," Catherine added.

The four middle managers who had been recently appointed to the customer service steering committee were surprised by Mark's and Catherine's relaxed joviality, but found it a relief to their own seriousness. They saw their assignment as an honor and an opportunity, but they were also apprehensive: their performance—or the way it was portrayed—could have an enduring impact on their reputations and careers.

"We're delighted that you have agreed to participate on the customer service steering committee," Mark said.

"We came to understand, as we previously stated, that the management team, working alone, cannot improve customer service. We must work with you and everyone else in the organization. This is a fact of life. Thus, we want you to help us involve everyone at Western Security in what we believe can be a vital and fun enterprise." Mark proceeded by introducing Catherine as the steering committee's executive liaison.

"The other department heads and Mark want to meet with this group, but we thought it was good for you to have a formal link to them, and that's me," Catherine began. She explained that she did not expect to be included every time they met, but they could take the initiative to meet with her, or she with them, whenever it seemed appropriate.

"We thought you should have some time to get to know each other better, establish yourselves as a team, and brainstorm ideas without members of the executive committee casting a shadow or talking too much," Mark said. "Are there any questions before I leave? We're literally depending on you to develop us as a company. I'm not being altruistic when I wish you the best of luck."

Catherine handed out the results of Western Security's customer service survey and told the steering committee that the executive committee had taken these results very seriously, committing themselves to improvement. She reminded the team members of their central function: to develop ways of involving everyone in improving customer service at Western Security.

"I'm not sure I completely understand," said Andre Tuzzard, a manager from the human resources department. With twenty-four years of service, he had one of the longest tenures of any employee in the organization. "You say you want us to decide the next steps, but on what basis are we to do this?"

Martina van der Werff from marketing, Edmund

Chua from operations, and Mike Dossa from accounting all joined in the discussion about their respective
roles and authority. At the end they understood more
clearly that their power would come from the strength
of their recommendations. The executive committee
would still be making the major decisions, but it was
relying on the steering committee to develop a program everyone could believe in.

Now it was Catherine's turn to wish them good luck
and leave.

"Right!" Edmund said with a hint of sarcasm. "This
is either an act of great leadership or an abdication.
I'm not sure which."

"I guess the executives would call this empowerment,"
Andre said.

"I think we've been handed something very exciting,
but it's kind of vague," said Mike.

"We've been called upon to do something extraordinary," Martina said. She had experienced more than her
share of personal and career struggles and saw her life
as a drama of obstacles and choices. She could bring
great determination and focus to a task.

While they had the usual prejudices against other
departments and did not know each other well, none
of the team members brought any personal antagonisms
and rivalries to the table. They could all see that they
shared an important task. Perhaps this would be one
of those lucky groups that somehow hit it off and develop good chemistry.

After letting off tension with banter and laughter,
they got down to business by discussing the principles
the executive committee had developed. The executives, they agreed, seemed committed to improving
customer service.

Martina wanted to show her enthusiasm. "I'm
excited that we have the top people so committed to
our customers. Customers keep us in business. It's
tough out there trying to keep the competition from
taking our customers."

"The trouble is that our employees have been subject to these scare tactics before," Edmund said. "You can only cry wolf so many times before people stop believing you."

"But we're not crying wolf," Martina said. "There's real danger; competition and the threat of losing customers are not imaginary."

"What Edmund's getting at is, I think, that people in the company may believe we're crying wolf," Mike said.

"Then we have to get them to understand that there are real dangers," Martina said.

"Bingo," Edmund said. "They've got to see for themselves."

"But we also want them to see the upside to this," Martina said. "That serving customers is fun."

"Now that might be a harder sell," said Andre. "You should hear the complaints I get from tellers about how customers treat them."

"I don't think we want to tell our people that they have to give more and do more," Mike said, looking at Martina. "Most of them think they're overworked and underpaid now."

"But we have to serve our customers," Martina said.

"I agree with both of you," said Edmund. "Somehow we have to make serving our customers rewarding. We can't just demand that our employees do it."

"Look at these survey results," Andre said. "I can see where they got Mark's attention."

While they saw how the results might have shocked the executives, they were not surprised. They decided to pass out a summary of the results so that employees could see for themselves why Western Security needed to invest in improving customer service.

"It's fine to talk about the value of serving customers, that we are not doing so well, and why we need to get better at it," Edmund said. "But the question is, how are we going to do it?"

"The easy part is deciding what the ideal is, the hard part is getting there," Andre said.

"That's where Mark's last two comments come in," Mike said. "We need involvement and teamwork to serve our customers better."

"That may be the right answer," said Edmund, "but it's not a very specific one."

"We're back to the rationale for our steering committee," Mike said. "How can we get people to see the need to serve customers?"

"Not only see the need, but feel passionate about it," Martina said.

"Can someone really feel passionate about serving others?" said Andre. "I mean it's a demanding and demeaning role."

"No! No! No!" said Martina, without rancor. "Helping people is a noble thing; serving them is an opportunity to be humane and compassionate. We're not going to get very far with the idea that serving customers is demeaning."

"Employees have to see that service has real value to them as well as to the customer," Edmund said.

"And they have to see how we can all work together to deliver," said Mike.

The group felt it had gotten a good fix on the challenge, and everyone felt more comfortable with each other. But the hard part was next: how should they proceed?

After kicking around a few ideas, Martina said, "Let's propose a change of the hierarchy so that customers are on top, the service providers are below them, and then supervisors, managers, and executives at the bottom."

"I've heard some very good companies use that model to emphasize how important serving customers is," Andre said.

"It does shake up people's assumptions," said Edmund.

"Frankly, I don't like this inversion," Mike said. "It gives the impression that customers and frontline people are bosses and the rest of us are supposed to take orders."

"It may also convey to the tellers and loan officers that they have to take orders from customers," Andre agreed. "Well, no one would believe us, anyway: the boss is still the boss."

"Come to think of it, putting customers on top doesn't suggest that working with customers can be fun, and it doesn't give an accurate view of the give-and-take of selling and marketing," Martina said.

"I don't think we want to communicate that we want to restructure the organization," Edmund said. "Talk about changing the structure is apt to be interpreted as another power game in which employees are pawns."

"We want to change values and attitudes more than lines of authority," said Andre.

The team realized that it was not going to be easy to decide how they could proceed. They set a meeting in ten days and agreed to be thinking, talking, and reading about customer service.

Edmund had come across an article applying the lessons of just-in-time manufacturing to service industries, and he sent copies to the steering committee members. (See summary of article, p. 63.)

At the beginning of the next meeting Edmund told the group, "I got excited about the pull versus the push approach to thinking about serving customers and talked with some friends in manufacturing who are using just-in-time." He explained that in the pull approach to production, a company organizes itself around the interests and demands of customers and "pulls in" people and resources, as needed, to serve them. In the traditional push system, the company organizes itself around the interests and demands of production: after one section completes its work on a product it "pushes" it on to the next workstation to be further processed until, eventually, the customer receives it.

"We use the push system, I think," Mike said.

"People who apply for a loan are asked to wait while the application goes through the various groups and levels to get the necessary approvals. But that's the way it has to be."

"We've got to be efficient," Andre said. "We can't expect our staff to be waiting around so that they are always free when a customer happens to want help."

"Maybe we can't, but maybe we can't afford to have customers waiting either. The push system assumes that customers are willing to wait and endure costs because the competition makes them do the same thing," said Edmund. "But in a world of intense competition, customers have lots of choices and high expectations, and these expectations are realistic because some companies will meet them."

"Well put, Edmund," Martina said. "You should make that speech to our employees. I bet it would get them fired up."

"The implications of this pull system seem subtle and huge at the same time," Edmund continued. "In the pull system, we're never allowed to lose track of the task of serving customers."

"Right now, we have people responsible and trained to do a specific function," said Andre. "They are expected to do their own job well. Would that have to change?"

"Well, from a push perspective, that's what you want," Edmund said. "But from a pull perspective, having everyone focused on their own individual task is a problem."

"Doing one's job seems so natural, though," Andre said. "We want people to take pride in that. We want them to do their own job well, not to worry about everyone else's job. How many times have we said this to our employees?"

"But how many times have we heard that we can't get people to do things that they don't feel responsible for?" Mike said. "We all complain about the 'don't blame me, that's someone else's job' syndrome."

"I get that all the time: 'We're okay, it's the other people who screwed up,'" said Martina.

"The pull system necessitates a much more fluid, dynamic type of organization rather than one with defined roles," said Andre.

"I can imagine employees having fun doing a variety of jobs — not just one boring one all day long," Martina said.

"But I can also imagine them talking about how they need a union to protect them from having too many responsibilities," said Andre. "One word about unionizing will throw the executives into panic."

"The executives won't go for raising wages, either," Edmund said. "I can hear them now talking about losing our competitiveness."

"Of course, if the employees wanted to learn to be able to switch jobs, then we would have a much different scenario," Andre said.

"We're back to the issue of using teamwork to improve how we serve our customers," Mike added.

"I'm a little frustrated," Martina said. "I mean, don't get me wrong: I've enjoyed our discussion, but we haven't made much progress. We all sort of knew that teamwork was what was needed, that we can't just tell people to serve customers. But how can we get our people to work together?"

## Moving Away from Push

Western Security Bank, like many other organizations, had witnessed dramatic changes in the marketplace. When the bank opened in 1947, the number of competitors was strictly limited by state regulations. The bank drew its customers from the local area it was designated to serve. Consumers expected to bank in their neighborhood with people who knew and appreciated them. Recently, however, technological advances, deregulation, and increased competition from other financial institutions have given consumers many more choices.

The push system of organizing was sensible when consumers had fewer choices and were content to receive a product of reasonable cost and quality. The push organization is configured for the efficient division and coordination of labor. Research and development creates a new product. Marketing estimates the demand for the product and plans how to attract customers. Production makes the product as efficiently as possible, and sales sells it. Each department, in turn, breaks its large task down into parts for individuals to do.

However, the push system is not as efficient as it first appears. It uses a considerable amount of materials because stations accumulate work to be processed. Bottlenecks easily occur in which one station is overloaded and cannot provide enough product to keep the station downstream operating efficiently. In service industries such as banks, people who are tired of waiting in lines may well take their business to the competition. Many opportunities are lost when employees are not fully engaged in the tailoring, producing, and marketing of products to customers.

## Pulling Together to Innovate

The push approach to product innovation has dominated organizational practice for decades. Research and development develops an idea, then "throws a prototype over the wall" to engineers who, in turn, throw it to manufacturing, purchasing, and marketing. The new product gets pushed through departments and layers of authority and is then handed over to salespeople, often years later, who are expected to push the product on to customers.

The pull approach is to form multidisciplinary teams that include people from all the areas required for developing and marketing a project successfully. These teams listen to customers' needs and ask for their ideas in developing new products. They involve suppliers in efforts to lower costs and improve quality. They survey the competition's offerings to determine realistic standards for the new product's performance.

The following list highlights the differences between the push and pull systems of management.

| Push | Pull |
|---|---|
| Employees are assigned specific tasks and are responsible for performing those tasks well. | Employees are united behind the vision of delivering quality service to customers. |
| Individuals are the basic building blocks of the organization. | Teams are the basic building blocks of the organization. |
| Complementary roles, written rules, and standard procedures are used to coordinate jobs and tasks. | Team members meet to decide how to coordinate jobs and tasks. |
| Managers make decisions and solve problems | Managers involve employees in solving problems and improving service. |
| Service providers interact with customers and protect the operating core. | All employees see themselves as service providers; as such, they are responsible for winning and keeping customers. |
| The marketing department works on its own to develop a strategy that attracts customers. | The marketing department involves the whole company in implementing strategy. |
| Customers are expected to build confidence and develop loyalty to the company on the basis of the company's reputation, the quality of its products, and the sales skills of frontline employees. | Customers are expected to build confidence and develop loyalty to the company on the basis of their relationship with employees, their confidence in the operations of the company, and the quality of the company's products. |

## Case Study:
## Milacron Pulls Ahead of the Competition

Milacron, a Cincinnati-based plastics machinery company, had been gaining sales during the early 1980s' growth market (Nultry, 1990). The rosy sales figures, though, masked the fact that they were losing market share to Japanese firms. Indeed, as market growth slowed, only five of the fifteen U.S. plastics machinery firms survived the 1980s.

Bruce Kozak, Micacron's sales representative in California, and Harold Faig, a product manager, were talking shop on a Sunday morning. Kozak said he was scared because Japanese machines were greatly outperforming and outselling their own. What they needed, they decided, was a new machine that would be 40 percent cheaper and would function at speed and operating times 40 percent better than their present one. And they needed the machine in one year, not two years, as was customary.

Kozak, Faig, and eight other men and one woman became the Project 270 team. Their first task was to talk with customers and examine rival machines. They were appalled. Japanese machines were much cheaper and could arrive the next day, not months later, as Milacron's might. American companies complained that their only sensible choice was to buy Japanese machines.

Milacron team members galvanized into action. They moved their offices close together and met every Monday. But decisions were not postponed until the meeting: their rule was to "make decisions daily."

Another precept that emerged was "no sacred cows." They changed from English to metric measurements to make the machine a world-class product. They broke tradition in using cast iron rather than plate steel and in promising to make suppliers their single source in exchange for providing them with high-quality materials and delivering quickly.

As the deadline approached, the cost of the new product was 35 percent lower than its predecessor's. Faig said that was unacceptable, and the team returned to work to squeeze another 5 percent from costs. After a slow first few months, late in 1986, demand for the new machine, renamed the Vista, mushroomed. In the first year, Milacron sold two and a half times more of the Vista than it ever had of any other machine. Even Japanese companies bought Vistas. And Milacron bought the idea of multidisciplinary pull teams and used them to upgrade other products.

---

### Special Focus: Just-In-Time for Service Companies

James A. Fitzsimmons (1990) proposed that the lessons of just-in-time (JIT) could be applied to service as well as manufacturing companies. JIT is a vehicle for developing the teamwork needed to solve ongoing problems and improve service to customers, providing high quality at the lowest possible cost.

The goal of JIT is to produce goods without storing inventory. Work arrives at a production station just as needed, instead of accumulating until it can be processed. A machine operator, for example, does not have a large queue of parts waiting to be processed, but receives work from a previous station "just-in-time" to process it.

In traditional methods, inventories of materials keep operators operating their machines continuously, since there is a built-up supply of work. In addition to considerable investment in materials, this system requires long production runs because of the high costs of changing set-ups. As a consequence, the company must also carry large inventories of completed work.

JIT's drive toward zero inventory challenges the production system; excess inventories cannot be used to hide problems. Defects in manufacturing are not lost in long assembly lines of products but are spotted very quickly; a defective part causes the next operator to wait for the defect to be corrected before continuing work. Employees are then asked to find ways to reduce defects and in other ways become allies with production engineers and other staff specialists to improve the production system. JIT frees and unites workers in a common effort to reduce costs and improve quality.

Service industries use waiting lines the way manufacturers use inventories—to hide problems. Customers must wait in lines for bank tellers because managers do not want to hire more tellers and have them idle when customer demand is low. Managers can hire and pay employees to perform specific tasks, and keep them busy, but if long waiting lines are forming for tellers, the bank and its customers are poorly served. As Fitzsimmons (1990) argues, excess inventories are costly indications that management is failing to stimulate the teamwork and continual improvement necessary to compete effectively.

The most devastating cost of waiting lines is the loss of future business. People will go where their time and their business seem more valued and respected. They may also conclude that such a poorly organized company is not likely to have the technical competence to provide high-quality service. Waiting lines, like excess inventory, also require space—beautiful atriums and long driveways for the drive-in bank—which also costs money.

JIT requires that a company's management and its culture foster employee involvement and teamwork for ongoing improvement. Rather than making decisions about what each worker should do, management should encourage employees to recognize that excess inventories and waiting lines are problems they need to solve. Waiting lines at a bank may alert loan officers and others to open up additional teller lines. When there are few customers, bank tellers can help their colleagues. Or perhaps a designated employee can greet and lead the customer to a specialist who is available and equipped to serve the customer's particular needs.

In JIT organizations, assumptions about how production is controlled and directed contrast sharply with the traditional model. In traditional organizations, work is "pushed" from one stage of production to the next. An operator processes the material and adds it to the stockpile of the next operator. In JIT, the final product desired is the beginning point and work is "pulled " from different operators as needed. Operators are continually focused on the final product and clearly see how they must work together to be successful. In a service company, the receptionist might be the first to become aware of customer demand and can alert service providers. In this way, customers "pull" resources into play to meet their needs.

Working together to serve customers and solve problems requires new thinking about organizations and new ways of managing. Technology must be used to assist service delivery, not to replace human contact. The focus of the company must be on serving the individual needs of customers, not on mass-marketing products and services. To be flexible, restrictive rules and role definitions must be replaced with more openness and fluidity. Employees can be hired and trained to do more than one job, and encouraged to work as a team. They all become service providers and ambassadors for the company; such important roles should not be restricted to the marketing department. Extensive cross-training, in turn, requires a greater commitment to and respect for employees. Management must no longer rely on the use of high-turnover and minimum-wage labor to serve customers. No longer enjoined to supervise and check, managers can, instead, coach, assist, and build teams.

---

## Moving to Pull

Edmund and the other steering committee members at Western Security were realizing that the pull concept of organization had far-reaching implications. They saw that changing into a pull organization would not be easy: it would be an ongoing journey, not a two-step process. Though their values pervade contemporary corporate culture, traditional push organizations are showing signs of strain. Savvy managers are experimenting with new product teams, interdepartmental task forces, and multiskilled work teams in the drive for higher quality, lower costs, and faster delivery to customers. However, managers and employees need a new way of thinking about organizations and working in them to make these new forums and procedures effective.

The pull organization promotes new attitudes, values, and skills and requires changes in the organization's roles and structures. Through dialogue and debates, not decrees, employees and managers work together to incorporate new values and create the forums that are effective and appropriate for them.

Teamwork is essential in a company that pulls out its resources and abilities to meet the particular needs of customers. But managers and employees are confused about the nature of productive teamwork and have few guidelines for creating it. The next chapter summarizes research on the nature of effective teamwork and indicates how this teamwork can be put into place according to the team organization model.

5

# Building Relationships:
# Elements of the
# Team-based Organization

*There is nothing so practical as a good theory.*

−Kurt Lewin

"I can see the light at the end of the tunnel," Martina said. The steering committee was just gathering for its third meeting, and she wanted to share her enthusiasm for the task and for the group.

"We are digging away," Edmund said with a laugh.

"We could just be burying ourselves," said Andre.

"Maybe we're scratching more than digging," Mike said. "But seriously, I really think we're making headway."

Mike went on to summarize the group's progress. They had agreed that employees must be fully involved so that they understand the need to improve customer service and use team problem solving and coordination to become a high-quality service company.

"Teamwork seems to be in fashion these days in management guru circles, but we need to give this a close look," said Andre. He had been trying to put his finger on what bothered him about last meeting's emphasis on teamwork. "We may be accused of sloganizing.

**67**

I can see employees' eyes glazing over as they think, 'Here comes the schlock again.'"

"Teamwork is like serving customers," Martina said. "Employees have to see that teamwork is valuable to them, that they're going to benefit from it."

"The company will benefit, no doubt, but will individuals?" asked Andre.

"If the company benefits, then individual employees benefit," Martina replied.

"They do?" Andre asked. "But not everyone can be promoted, and some people will be promoted just because they're team players."

"Andre has a point, but so does Martina," said Edmund. "If the company goes under, people don't have to worry about promotions."

"But we should know whether teamwork is really good for people, beyond any benefit to the company," Mike said. "We want to be credible when we talk to employees. I always think that getting on well with people at work makes coming to work a lot more rewarding, but that may just be me. We need some research."

"There's an even larger problem," said Andre. "Do we really know what teamwork is?"

"Relationships, teamwork—these are 'soft' topics to be sure," said Edmund.

"But they're basic," Martina said. "Teamwork simply means people are honest with each other, respect each other, help each other out, get along. We're talking kindergarten here."

"Let me point out that most people believe these things and talk about them, but have a tough time practicing them," Andre said.

"Even the so-called experts don't agree on teamwork," Mike said. "Some say you're supposed to let it all hang out and others tell you to listen more and get along. I heard one family therapist talk about how couples should fight more. She made sense at the time."

For the rest of the meeting they discussed the value and nature of productive teamwork. They agreed they needed to do some research to get a handle on the elusive phenomenon of teamwork. They agreed to search for and distribute articles and books on the topic before their next meeting.

"I like the team organization model that I had sent around," Mike said at the beginning of the next session. "The model is supposed to tell us the nature of productive teamwork in an organization and how to develop it."

"That's the one where a group's cycle of activities is represented in a circle, right?" Edmund asked [see Figure 1.1].

"Yes," said Mike. "Effective teams envision a common direction, feel united behind this vision, empower each other to act with confidence, explore opposing positions to solve problems, and reflect on their experiences and continue to grow."

"How would this apply to our group?" asked Edmund.

"Let's see." Mike thought for a moment. "Our vision is to guide Western Security to be a customer-friendly bank; we are united in our commitment to it; we are empowered by our reading and group discussions; and we are certainly exploring different pathways and possibilities. The reflect part, I think, is recognizing our progress and managing our conflicts, which I guess we're doing, though we haven't had many conflicts yet."

"Interesting ideas," said Martina. "But I'm afraid my study skills are rusty; it's going to take me a while to get my mind around this model."

"I know what you mean," Mike said. "The authors talk about learning and applying the model as a group. They want employees and managers to discuss the model together and then decide how to implement changes so that they become a team. The method is the message."

"But first things first," said Andre. "We still haven't decided if we can really tell people at Western Security that this or any other kind of teamwork is good for them."

"I've been looking for an answer ever since the last meeting," Martina said. "What I've learned is that teamwork is good for people because it helps them be themselves. They can be supported by others while achieving goals and accomplishing tasks."

"It's like you can't fully express your individuality without others to help you," said Mike. "It seems like an odd idea at first, but it's beginning to make more sense."

"For our group, for example, you have to admit that it would be much more difficult and much less fun for only one of us to think about how Western Security could be customer-responsive," Edmund said.

"It would never get done," Martina said.

"But we all know that groups suppress people and sink to the lowest common denominator, etc., etc.," said Andre.

"Some groups do and some groups don't," Mike said. "That's why we need to make teamwork effective so that people are encouraged to express their views, manage their conflicts, and be themselves."

"That's another interesting idea I got from the reading," said Martina. "People in a team are eventually going to disagree, and it's necessary to discuss these conflicts."

"I'm not trying to be a troublemaker," said Andre, "but is this model supposed to apply to all groups? I mean, our group is different than a group of bank tellers."

"The model, as I understand it, is supposed to be a general one," Mike said. "The authors argue that the model summarizes a great deal of theory and research, but that people can apply it so that it fits their needs."

"Does anyone else feel we need to study this model more?" asked Andre.

"I do," Martina said. "You've gotten us off to a good start. But we need more time to discuss and criticize the model if we are going to use it."

Edmund nodded in agreement. "It's not enough for us to write memos telling everyone to work as a team. We need to give them a picture, a set of guides, for how they can work as a team."

"As Martina said, we must all believe that this kind of teamwork will pay off," said Mike.

"And to believe in teamwork, we have to understand what it is and how it is useful," Andre said.

## The Components of Team Organization

The top management and the steering committee at Western Security had begun to discuss their views openly, dig into issues, and work together successfully. The executives had their personal rivalries but were ready for a more open and productive way of working together, and Mark was able to model the way. Not every group finds such a straightforward path to collaboration. Knowledge about the nature of effective teamwork is essential when rallying the organization, and the departments within it, to work together.

Successful teamwork is one thing and many things (Tjosvold, 1986, 1991b). There is no step that, in itself, makes a team productive. In a team organization, people throughout the organization are committed to their common vision, are united behind the vision, are empowered to work together to realize it, are willing to explore issues and decisions by considering opposing views, and are able to reflect on their conflicts and their progress.

These aspects of teamwork complement and supplement each other. Teams that have a vision and feel united also have more confidence that they can be successful and are better able to explore different points of view. They look for ways to learn from their experiences and improve how they work together to make their vision a reality.

## Envision: Our Direction

A clear, compelling direction is critical to developing a team and organization. All members must be fully aware of the team's strategic plan, code of ethics, and organizational structure. They must know what they are expected to accomplish and how they will work together to achieve it. They must understand the importance of this vision for themselves and others, and be committed to pursuing it. It is the vision which motivates and directs. As Seneca wrote, "If a man does not know to which port he is sailing, no wind is favorable."

Visions do not just appear; they must be created. Effective leaders look beyond the everyday distractions of work to ponder the future. Leaders are pioneers who challenge the status quo and are willing to risk failure to search for a better way (Kouzes & Posner, 1987). Though not necessarily innovators, they recognize good ideas and work to get them implemented.

Yet leaders cannot create the vision alone. They must incorporate employee concerns and ideas in creating the group's vision. They need to enlist employees to help them mold the vision. Ideally, they realize they cannot demand commitment — they must inspire it. Leaders are "keepers of the dream," as Steve Jobs said, but they must inspire others to share this dream.

Creating a shared vision involves a number of different steps, which may include

- *Assessing the team's present vision.* Customers, industry experts, and competitors can help team members examine the present strategy and assess its viability and risks.
- *Reflecting on customer service.* Collecting and analyzing information on service delivery and customer experiences and opinions can suggest new directions and galvanize action.
- *Reflecting on the organizational framework.* Employees can discuss

the nature of productive teamwork and compare their work relationships to the team organization model. Then they can commit themselves to working as a team.

- *Confronting relationship issues.* Dealing directly with grievances and conflicts is essential to forging a common vision. When management encourages people to discuss problems and pursue resolution it helps foster cooperative relationships throughout the organization. These relationships form the foundation upon which teamwork is built.
- *Searching for opportunities to initiate change, innovation, and growth.* Rather than wait for a crisis to hit, the team looks for things that are "broken" and fixes them. They can challenge the routine, making their work an enjoyable adventure. When employees examine their concerns about the business strategy and discuss the things that annoy them about their jobs and environment, they participate in the management of their team. With everyone participating, there is a greater flow of ideas and more personal investment in success.
- *Taking risks and learning from mistakes.* People must gather new ideas and experiment with them.
- *Developing and presenting a short statement that outlines the vision.* Powerful and unifying, this statement can evoke images and metaphors in describing the company's mission and philosophy.
- *Evaluating the vision.* Team members can discuss the ways in which the company code of ethics and value system do and do not support the strategy and organizational framework.
- *Updating the vision.* The team can revise its vision in light of internal and external changes. It must listen again and again to customers' ideas and complaints, industry experts' predictions, and the competition's claims.
- *Appreciating accomplishments.* The team should celebrate its capacity to change and reward its own progress. A newsletter prepared by team members can summarize progress toward achieving the vision and keep all employees interested and involved.

## Unite: We Are Together

A compelling vision unites team members in a common effort. Sensing they are moving in the same direction, they communicate openly and understand each other. They realize they need the information, knowledge, ideas, support, and energy of others to get their jobs done and to contribute successfully to the company. They have, in the words of Alexandre Dumas, a feeling of "all for one, one for all."

Cooperative unity cannot be taken for granted. Even a vision to serve customers is no guarantee of quality service. Employees might believe that they should compete against each other to show the boss they are the most able to serve customers. They may want to prove to themselves that they are better than others. Furthermore, cooperative work, at times, seems impractical and costly. Employees often would rather work on their own individual tasks than take time from a busy day to coordinate efforts. The costs of attending another meeting or rearranging vacation time often seem very immediate, whereas the benefits of working together to develop a new program can seem very distant.

Nor can unity be decreed. It is not enough for managers to talk about how employees should cooperate, or blame them for not doing so. People must come to their own conclusion that what is good for one is good for all; success for one is success for all. Moreover, cooperative interdependence needs everyone's participation. One person cannot cooperate alone. Everybody must see the goals and be willing to work with others to accomplish them.

There are a variety of ways to promote cooperative teamwork. The following list can serve as a guideline.

- *Keep track of group productivity.* All workers average their individual output to form a group average for each week. Each worker is responsible for keeping his or her output up, and for helping others improve theirs.
- *Promote group learning.* All group members are expected to improve their skills in working with people, selling, and

operating machinery and to help each other learn. The manager will choose at random one team member to demonstrate learning, and the team is rated on that basis.

- *Praise the team as a whole for its success.* The manager recognizes all members of the team and their accomplishments are written up in the company newsletter.
- *Reward individuals based on group performance.* Each team member receives a monetary bonus based on the team's success.
- *Hold an unproductive group accountable for its actions.* Managers confront failed teams and have them suffer some consequence, rather than single out an individual to blame.
- *Make the task challenging.* Team members will be highly motivated to accomplish achievable but difficult tasks and will recognize they need everyone's ability and support to do so.
- *Assign complementary roles.* One employee is asked to record ideas, another to encourage full participation, another to be a devil's advocate to challenge common views, and a fourth to observe and provide feedback to help the group reflect on its workings.
- *Encourage team identity.* Teams devise and publicize their own name and symbol. Members focus on their common characteristics and backgrounds.
- *Promote personal relationships.* Team members discuss their feelings and values they consider important. "Small talk" about family and oneself develops personal, trusting relationships. Social gatherings such as Friday afternoon "beer busts" and Christmas parties encourage such interaction.
- *Write a statement of values and ethics.* Team members develop their own value statement. These values emphasize that they belong together, care about each other, and should be helpful "citizens." Employees recall stories and examples that illustrate the vision, values, norms, and unity of the team.

### Empower: We Can Do It

Feeling united in a common effort contributes to the team's confidence that the vision can be realized. However, team members do not exert themselves fully unless they know that they have the skills, technical resources, and organizational mandate to combine their ideas and efforts successfully. Empowering, like envisioning and uniting, cannot be done to people; it is a process in which all must participate. But the payoff can be considerable. A Chinese proverb reminds us, "If you want one year of prosperity, grow grain. If you want ten years of prosperity, grow trees. If you want one hundred years of prosperity, grow people."

Teams are not islands. They need the organization's mandate, permission, and support to be highly effective. The company must provide new product teams with the time, money, and other resources they need to do their job. Team members must also believe that management will approve the production and marketing of their product if it meets requirements. Without such expectations, team members feel there is no point in trying.

Central to a sense of power and confidence is the knowledge that team members have the necessary technical skills and resources to reach the group goal. When the new product team members believe they have all the research, development, industrial engineering, production, and marketing expertise they need within their group, they are enthusiastic about joining forces in a common effort.

Interpersonal and social skills are also vital to productive teamwork. Working together requires sensitivity, empathy, and confrontation. People need to be aware of the feelings and needs of others, and respond to them. They must exchange information and, at times, challenge each other's position and thinking. If team members believe that meetings will be unproductive and unpleasant because of indifference or acrimony, they will not have much enthusiasm about attending, although they need team meetings and gatherings to exchange ideas and assist each other.

Individual responsibility and team accountability empower a group. Employees do not want others to get a "free ride" while they end up doing all the work. People avoid situations in which they suspect that they will be unjustly exploited. Team members need to divide the labor fairly and effectively. They must feel a sense of personal accountability, motivating them to complete their tasks so that other team members can complete theirs.

They must do their own jobs and whatever else it takes to make the team enterprise successful.

People who are specialists in technical areas, facilitating groups, and linking with management will all help the team accomplish its goals. Team members should discuss their previous accomplishments, experiences, and credentials, and in other ways disclose their personal strengths, so that their skills and talents are put to full use. Team members can also hold each other accountable to the group by reporting on their various activities. Individuals who complete their assignments may be praised or rewarded; individuals who fail to fulfill their obligations may be offered assistance if necessary, or they may be reprimanded and even punished.

Team members can keep current in their specialties by taking courses, reading books and journals, and discussing ideas. Readings, workshops, and reflection on experiences develop skills in dealing with conflicts and other group issues. Regular meetings, having offices close together, electronic mail, and computer systems help team members exchange information and keep each other posted.

The organization that rewards group effort, uses teamwork as a criterion for promotion, provides training in group skills, and makes consultation on teamwork available is likely to develop a culture of spirited teamwork. On the other hand, if management second guesses decisions and allows teams little autonomy to experiment with new ways of working, the team will not accept responsibility for its actions or feel empowered to effect change, and teamwork will eventually unravel.

### Explore: We Use Our Diversity

Working together and feeling empowered do not mean smooth sailing and inevitable success. Teams hit bumps and get bruises along the way. Every group needs the ability to identify issues, explore them, and overcome barriers to move toward its vision. Teams must be able to discuss their opposing views openly to solve problems and make decisions. Alfred Sloan, as chair of General Motors, once advised his executive team, "I take it we are all in complete agreement on the decision here. . . . Then I propose we postpone further discussion until our next meeting to give ourselves time to develop disagreement and perhaps gain some understanding of what the decision is all about" (Drucker, 1974).

Issues and decisions come in such a great variety that there is no way in particular that they should be approached. The first rule is that the team must be flexible and use the approach appropriate for the situation. At times, decisions must be made quickly with little or no consultation. A leader or coordinator can dispense with minor issues efficiently. Other decisions are not worth the effort to explore in great depth, and previous solutions can be reasonably applied.

However, what is critical is how the team approaches decisions about important, ongoing issues, for these are the ones that give the group its character and impact. In dealing with such issues, the team should explore the problems, create alternatives, and choose a high-quality solution that strengthens the group.

The second rule of decision making is that teams need to promote constructive controversy to explore issues and alternatives. Differences of opinion can temporarily prevent or delay reaching a decision. When constructively handled, however, this controversy contributes substantially to successful teamwork (Tjosvold, 1985a, 1987).

Through controversy, people become open to new information and oposing viewpoints. Confrontation causes people to doubt their own position. They become interested in opponents' arguments and ask questions to explore it. Thus, they develop a more complex and accurate view of the problem and incorporate opposing views into their decisions. Controversy creates new solutions by integrating a range of seemingly contradictory ideas. People appreciate the issues more completely and are committed to implementing the solution because they understand its rationale and purpose.

To be successful, controversy must reaffirm a team's unity and empowerment. Competitive, win-lose discussions that attack people's abilities and motives are counterproductive. They tear teams apart and create defensive attitudes and ineffective solutions. Handled well, controversy can increase the trust and unity within a group.

Teams should explore issues thoroughly by protecting and stimulating diverse views. They can search for opposing ideas and integrate them to create workable situations. Following is a list of strategies for promoting healthy controversy.

- *Include diverse people.* Independent people who differ in background, expertise, opinions, outlook, and organizational position are likely to disagree.
- *Establish norms for openness.* Everyone is encouraged to express his or her opinions, doubts, and hunches. Ideas are not dismissed because they appear too unusual, impractical, or undeveloped.
- *Protect rights.* The right to dissent and free speech reduces fears of retribution for speaking out.
- *Assign opposing views.* Coalitions are formed and given opposing positions to present and defend. One person is assigned a critical evaluation role in which he or she attacks the group's current preference.
- *Probe for opposing views.* Team members stop defending their own views long enough to ask each other for more information and arguments. They put themselves in each other's shoes by listening carefully and reflecting back the other's position and arguments.
- *Use the golden rule of controversy.* People act the way they want others to act: if they want other people to listen to them, then they must listen to other people.
- *Show personal regard.* People criticize ideas rather than attack an individual's motivation and personality. Insults or implications that challenge another's integrity, intelligence, and motives should be discouraged.

### Reflect: We Can Improve

Teams need to be able to assess their present state of functioning, celebrate and build upon their accomplishments, learn from mistakes, and deal with frustrations. Effective groups monitor and regulate themselves so that they can continue to work together without a great deal of manager intervention. They work to ensure that they will be productive in the future as well as the present. As Thomas Paine wrote, "I love the man who can smile in trouble, who can gather strength from distress, and who can grow brave by reflection."

Though it may appear permanent, the status quo is illusory. Kurt Lewin argued that the present state of affairs is a product of equilibrium — a temporary balance of forces. But these forces will inevitably change, affecting a team's outlook. There are, for example, forces that help them feel united, but also ones that push them apart. A sense of unity results from the balance of these forces. But one fight may convince people they cannot work together and undermine their confidence. Maintaining the status quo is seldom a real alternative: groups are either growing or declining.

An essential first step in planning for a productive future is to investigate and assess a group's present functioning (Argyris, 1970). Organization development specialists have created a rich array of methods for collecting data. Team members can complete a survey questionnaire and later receive a summary of the results. Through process consultation, a group is observed functioning. Any findings are discussed with the group to help them become more aware and effective. Interviewing team members individually can help clarify their perspectives and experiences. Group members as well as outside consultants can use these methods to assess the team's present dynamics. Of course, to be useful, the studies should focus on areas the group can influence. According to the team organization model, the best areas to assess are those that affect envisioning, uniting, empowering, and exploring.

Avoiding conflicts and smoothing over frustrations are not effective strategies for problem resolution. Indeed, dealing openly and directly with conflicts enables a group to maintain and strengthen itself. Through conflict, people become aware of their own and others' frustrations. They also discover where their vision, unity, empowerment, and exploration are deficient. Conflict creates the incentive and energy people need to deal with problems. Well-managed conflict is the medium in which teams grow.

An effective team does not appear quickly or easily; team members must think in terms of continuous improvement and ongoing development, not a one-stop quick fix.

The team organization model summarizes a great deal of research on goals, cooperation and competition, power, controversy, group processing, and conflict management (Tjosvold, 1991b). Documentation reveals that cooperative teamwork drives innovation and provides a rich, human experience binding people within an organization together.

The team organization model identifies the hurdles that individuals must overcome to become members of a high-performance team. Teamwork requires much. Employees must be committed to the organization's vision and task, united in their purpose, empowered to achieve, and able to explore opposing views and reflect on their experiences. But this spirited teamwork gives much to organizations and people. Through it, organizations can offer greater value to customers and provide rich rewards for serving customers well.

Companies intent on serving customers need a concise theory about effective teamwork, such as a team organization model. Without such a shared framework, people are often unsure about how they are supposed to interact and cooperate. As Kurt Lewin said, there is nothing so practical as a good theory, especially when people apply it together. The next part shows how people can study the team organization model and use it together to better serve customers.

*Part Three*

# CREATING
# AND
# SUSTAINING

*You cannot build character and courage by taking away men's initiative
and independence.
You cannot help men permanently by doing for them what they could
and should do for themselves.*

*—Abraham Lincoln*

The foundation for developing an organization that reaches out to its customers lies in developing service teams. Through discussing the team organization model, employees are able to deepen their understanding of teamwork and plan how to put it in place. Quality service cannot be decreed or forced, but comes out of a shared conviction in the value of working together to serve customers. Employees form teams in which they combine their expertise and insights to understand and act upon customer needs. Teams also help employees learn and develop new ways to improve customer service.

# 6

# Encouraging Teams:
# The Need
# for Leadership Support

*Tell me and I'll forget; show me and I may remember; involve me and I'll understand.*

*—Chinese proverb*

"I can see you are fired up about working as a team to serve customers," Catherine said to the steering committee. "That's great. The next hurdle is going to be getting the rest of the company equally enthusiastic."

"We've decided that we have to get the employees themselves to understand the need to invest in teamwork and customer service," said Edmund.

"I agree," Catherine said. "The old 'tell-and-sell' approach just doesn't work."

"We want employees to do what we've been doing," Mike said. "Studying and discussing customer service and teamwork."

"We can hand out readings, but that's not enough," said Andre. "Employees have to talk to each other about the issues and come to a consensus about where and how we should proceed."

They discussed how the steering committee could stimulate the interest and debate needed to move

Western Security forward. They would check within
the human resources department and outside the company for people who could help them design a workshop.

With the assistance of a consultant, the steering
committee developed a plan for involving more employees in determining the new direction. After having
their plan approved by the executives, the committee
invited managers from all departments and units to a
two-day retreat on customer service and teamwork. In
preparation for the retreat they sent the managers a
summary of the customer service survey results and
readings on customer service, push and pull organizations, and team organization. Steering committee
members also talked informally with participants, answering questions about the upcoming event and
stimulating interest.

Participants were excited as they gathered at the
workshop hotel, though some were still reluctant to
believe that Western Security could move forward
decisively. The steering committee was both eager and
apprehensive. They felt a successful workshop could
have a great impact on Western Security, but they had
little experience conducting this kind of meeting.

After Catherine had introduced the steering committee, Mark talked about what had led to the decision to
appoint a steering committee on customer service and,
eventually, to have this retreat. "Customer service is
not something that we want to badger employees with.
Improving how we serve customers is very much a
'win-win.' The company benefits from having loyal
customers. We all benefit as people because serving
others is a most worthy—even noble—endeavor."

The managers wanted to believe that their branch
had a vital mission. Away from the everyday pressures
and in the presence of other upbeat managers, they
were moved by Mark's talk.

Next, Martina thanked Catherine and Mark and

asked that managers form groups of three. In their groups, managers discussed why improving customer service was important to Western Security and its employees. Managers started to see the concrete benefits of improving customer service, not just for the customers, but for the company and for themselves, as well.

Mike introduced the next issue. "We need teamwork if we're going to decide how we can best serve our customers and actually deliver for them. We have a simple plan: you work. This is a *work*shop, and you're not just going to be listening to inspiring talks."

"And we were just beginning to think highly of you," said one manager to general laughter.

The plan was to use the jigsaw method, dividing managers into five groups. Each group was responsible for learning one aspect of the team organization model so that everyone in their group could teach others about it. Each group was given the model, a definition, and an outline for proceeding: envision, unite, empower, explore, and reflect. [See Chapter Five.] They were given twenty-five minutes to work.

When twenty-five minutes were up, Mike and Andre formed new groups of five, taking one person from each of the original five groups. They asked the managers to take turns being the focus person, teaching his or her part of the model so that everyone in the group understood it. Each person was to introduce the idea, discuss how it could be developed, and answer any questions. Andre asked the groups to discuss next how the different components of the model could reinforce each other. The groups were given forty minutes to complete these tasks, and when they were done everyone went to lunch.

After lunch, Edmund said, "Now that you have studied the team organization model, I want the same groups to take fifteen minutes to critique it and identify its weaknesses."

When the groups reported their findings they cited several weaknesses: the model did not provide a concrete program of action, was too complex to communicate quickly, and did not clearly define leaders' roles. Edmund reminded the managers that the model was meant to be a general guideline for encouraging productive teamwork and that how it was implemented would depend on their own skills and sensitivities.

Andre then asked these groups to brainstorm about ways that teamwork could help Western Security deliver value to customers. In response, the groups proposed that teamwork could help Western Security employees be more flexible and reduce waiting lines, develop new products, create a more upbeat atmosphere, teach new employees how to treat customers and deal with their complaints, and help frontline people be more open and helpful.

Martina arranged people into five new groups and asked each to focus on one aspect of the team organization model. The groups were asked to identify concrete ways Western Security employees could envision, unite, empower, explore, and reflect. The groups came back with quite a few ideas. They suggested that all employees should take part in workshops similar to this one so that they could develop an understanding of the value of customer service and teamwork. The company should also consider a company-wide bonus system tied to improved customer service. Employees should be trained in different jobs so that they could be more flexible in dealing with customers. Task forces could be formed to supply the many perspectives needed for solving company problems. Annual meetings with all employees could be used to reflect on progress and create strategy for the future. Western Security needed to move away from short-term crisis management and develop more long-term goals.

In the evening the managers were placed in new groups and asked to develop and act out skits showing how Western Security did not want to treat its customers and frontline employees. It was a night of

laughter and camaraderie, reminding all that Western
Security had much work to do in improving customer
service.

The next morning discussion was devoted to conflict
management. Edmund pointed out that there is a great
deal of potential for conflict when people work together
in teams. By managing their conflicts openly, he suggested, team members could use conflict to strengthen
their relationships and enhance their ability to work
together. If they practiced basic negotiation skills,
learned more about positive conflict, and used groups
to advocate different positions, they could use controversy to help make decisions (Tjosvold, 1991a, in
press).

In the afternoon, task forces were formed to deal
with specific assigned issues. One group focused on how
to create a shared vision for customer service and
teamwork. Another group discussed a bonus plan that
would foster teamwork. The remaining groups dealt
with the training of frontline personnel and the use
of technology.

Surprisingly, the presentation on the use of technology generated the most discussion. The presenting
group wanted to reconsider the proposed new information system. Though the new system might be fine for
the efficient handling of information, it was not
directly useful for improving customer service.

"You don't understand," said Peter. "The computer
system is designed to improve accuracy and reduce labor
costs."

"We understand that," said one of the group's
members with a smile. "When you propose something,
it usually involves reducing labor costs."

"It's a good, proven system," Peter said, trying to
state his position without sounding defensive.

"We don't disagree, but we know there are systems
that can do much more," said another manager. "Some
give bank tellers all the information about a customer

with a push of a button. They enable employees to tell customers exactly what their balance is, the status of their loans, when their certificates are due, and so forth, without having to run around the office to collect the information. Our tellers would be able to remind a customer to renew this certificate, call attention to a loan issue, or whatever."

"We're thinking that kind of information system would give bank tellers better opportunities to cross-sell services, too, as well as provide superior service," added another group member.

"Why didn't you tell me this earlier?" Peter asked jokingly.

"We just assumed that your sysem was the next logical step and never thought of questioning it," said a manager. "Then when we got together in this group, we came up with this other idea, and it seemed so sensible."

Peter did not like being surprised in front of so many people. Still, he knew he had not been intentionally embarrassed. "It's better to consider this idea now than five months down the road. We'll have to look into this." Then he smiled. "But what about that million hours of labor costs I was going to save . . ."

"Well," said Mark, "our time is just about up. How does the steering committee want us to proceed?"

"We thought we could recruit volunteers for task forces to help us move forward," Andre said.

"Yes, we could ask people from across the organization to form a task force on technology and customer service to make sure that our investment will help us get where we want to go," Mike said.

"We also would like to involve frontline employees and others, right?" Mark said.

"Sounds good," said Edmund.

Mark asked the mangers to join him in thanking the steering committee for its good work. The managers cheered, and the steering committee thanked and cheered the managers.

## Helping People Get on Track

Edmund, Mike, and other members of the steering committee were learning that commitment has to be nurtured; it cannot be commanded. It comes from understanding and belief, not external pressure. It develops through honest debate and conflict, not from elaborate speeches and fancy overheads.

"Tell and sell" is the traditional approach for trying to get employees committed to a company vision. They are deluged with fancy rhetoric and inspiring speeches. This approach is thought to be a cost-effective, practical way to reach a large group of people. However, one-way communication, through speeches and reading, is only a beginning. As the steering committee showed, there are other ways to reach a large group of people so that they develop a shared conviction to work together to serve customers.

The team organization model provides credible, consistent common ground for developing this shared conviction. People study, discuss, and critique the model together; they work as a team in order to strengthen themselves as a team. The method reinforces the message.

Western Security managers were adopting the team organization model as part of their vision for the company. They envisioned their company working as a team to serve customers and understood the value of this vision for the company and for themselves. They felt united behind that vision and expected everyone to contibute to their common success. They were empowering each other by learning about teamwork. Together they explored different ways that they could put team organization in place and improve customer service. They were reflecting on their experiences and committing themselves to ongoing improvement.

Learning about team organization involves action and experimentation as well as reading and discussion. Managers and employees used small cooperative groups to figure out how Western Security could use the model. The groups reexamined and refined the model while clarifying their thinking. Their deeper understanding will eventually lead to new action which, in turn, will lead to reflection, deeper understanding, and more effective action. In this way, theory informs action and action enlarges theory.

## Special Focus: The Jigsaw Method

Western Security managers and employees used a jigsaw method to understand the team organization model and learn how to apply it. Jigsawing involves grouping and re-grouping individuals to maximize interaction among them (Johnson & Johnson, 1989b; Tjosvold & Tjosvold, 1991).

First, five groups are formed and each one is given information and materials that relate to one component of the team organization model. Each group should have a maximum of ten people. If there are more than fifty people in the workshop, ten or more groups can be formed and more than one group can discuss each component.

Each group should be assigned the responsibility to become an expert in its part of the model. The groups ensure that all of the members understand and are prepared to teach their assigned part. People in the group share ideas and work together to develop the best approach for teaching their assigned component. Thus, they might develop a visual or some other teaching aid to give others a picture of their part of the model.

Next, one person from each of the five expert groups should form a learning group. Each person in the learning group is asked to teach his or her part and to learn the other parts of the team organization model. The group can then discuss how the components complement each other.

Finally, groups give presentations that demonstrate their understanding of the team organization model. They answer questions, discuss the model's limitations, and suggest how the model can be used in the organization.

Employed in this way, the jigsawing method can be used to deepen people's understanding of each part of the team organization model and to set teamwork in motion.

## Achieving Synergy

Western Security, like most organizations, was not so much a company as a collection of departments, and it was to their department that employees felt loyal. Departments initiated programs and made investments that would increase their efficiency. The system that Peter favored was geared to improving the efficiency of operations, thereby saving labor and money for the company. Although from Peter's perspective this reasoning was sensible, it was not optimal for the company as a whole.

Synergy across departmental and other lines is necessary for effective innovation. Improving customer service does not mean that the marketing department should be allowed to dominate the company. It is not wise to innovate in one part of the company as if it were independent of others. Excellence in serving customers requires the commitment of all departments so that diverse people forge integrated solutions to realize the company vision.

---

### Case Study:
### Innovation and Coordination at Interrent

The Swedish car rental company Interrent used teamwork throughout the company to improve their basic and auxiliary services (Gronroos, 1990). Facing increased competition, the company decided in 1986 to create a unique market position by offering trustworthy, reliable service, not just "we do it with a smile" or "we try harder" slogans. Top management decided on three service guarantees that extended the company's capacity.

The "get to the destination" guarantee meant that customers would be on the way to their destination within forty-five minutes of informing Interrent of a breakdown in service. In addition to maintaining the cars in good condition, local stations had to be prepared to act quickly to restore service. If no other solution could be reached, the customers would be delivered by taxi to their destination at company expense. Customers would have a twenty-four-hour telephone number to report a breakdown.

The "lowest price" guarantee meant that Interrent's computers would always quote the lowest possible fee for the customer. Customers no longer had to figure out how to get the best rates, whether they should rent a car on a daily basis or for a weekend, or whether they should choose a no-mileage fee or not.

"Trouble-free service" required that the customer be inconvenienced as little as possible. In addition to picking up and dropping off a car at any station, an Interrent car would be delivered to a company address, railway station, or hotel no later than five minutes after the agreed upon time, or the customer would not be billed. Traffic jams or other unexpected delays were not acceptable excuses.

CEO Hans Åke Sand and other managers faced the challenge of involving all employees in developing the abilities and resources to meet these guarantees. Not only did they need to be able to explain the guarantees to customers, frontline employees needed the autonomy, information, and computer technology to deliver the high-quality services. Marketing had to advertise the guarantees. Maintenance had to improve its car servicing to keep the cost of breakdowns to a minimum. Customers, too, had to participate by learning about the guarantees from advertisements, agents' explanations, and documentation in the cars.

Some Interrent managers and employees doubted that the commitments to "five-minute maximum delay" and "within forty-five minutes on the road again" were realistic and cost-effective. Service seminars involving the CEO and other top managers were held to discuss and debate the changes. Hans Åke Sand concluded that "the people in the organization perceived the total program we were to offer our customers as a challenge, but they also realized that the firm trusted them, and we achieved a commitment for the new service" (Gronroos, 1990, p. 89).

The results of this program were gratifying. In the first year, sales were 23 percent higher than the same period a year earlier. Much to the surprise of many, costs did not rise significantly. The program also had a positive impact on the organization itself. Because it was implemented through teamwork, the program's success strengthened company synergy.

---

Teams and departments throughout an organization must coordinate and work together effectively to deliver value to customers. Within this supportive environment, individuals and their teams are empowered to perform for and serve customers. The next chapter examines how teams that work directly with customers can be structured and nurtured.

# 7

# Forming Teams:
# New Structures
# for Service Efforts

"I want to make a difference," said Dan Milburn,
manager of the Maplewood branch of Western Security.
He had just outlined to the steering committee his proposal that Maplewood be the first branch to strengthen
teamwork and customer service.

"Good. We need enthusiastic volunteers," said Mike.
"Give us some time to think about your proposal, and
we'll get back to you."

Dan saw an opportunity. To him, the workshop had
demonstrated that Mark and the other executives were
genuinely committed to customer service and teamwork.
His staff liked the program Steve and Peter had used
to solicit their ideas about how a computer system could

help them serve customers. He wanted his branch to break new ground and implement the customer service program at the branch level. He wondered, though, why the steering committee seemed lukewarm to his proposal.

"I feel like I should be enthusiastic about Dan's proposal, but I'm not," said Edmund after Dan left. "What's your reaction?"

"I'm all for moving forward, and this pilot project at Maplewood seems plausible," Martina said. "But I'm afraid that Dan might alienate people in the other branches. I hope I'm not just being prejudiced against a young, ambitious man who lacks the right manners."

"I don't think it's that he went to the wrong finishing school," Mike said. "It's that he's not considered a team player. People think he's out for his own interests, not the company's."

"If he runs the pilot program, I can see other managers thinking this customer service idea is being thrown in their face," Andre said. "They'll think it's a competition to see who is the most cooperative and most committed to customers."

"We need to channel Dan's enthusiasm so that it is and is perceived to be a cooperative one," said Mike. "We've got to show that he and his branch are taking the lead to find out what works and what doesn't so that the other branches can learn and improve."

"I like that approach," Edmund said. "But how can we communicate it?"

"I'll talk to Dan," said Mike. "We owe it to him to talk straight and let him know our concerns. We want the project at Maplewood to be something that other branches will see as useful to them."

"Good. But we have another issue," Edmund said. "I'm not sure Maplewood has credibility because of its location in the poorer suburbs. It's not performing well. People might not take a success out there seriously."

"The credibility problems with Dan and Maplewood

are related," Andre said. "Dan got the job at Maplewood because managers thought he was too energetic
to let go, but didn't want to have to deal with him every day. So they sent him out to Maplewood."

"That's called management, I guess," Edmund said.
"Do we pay people real money to make decisions like
that?"

"We'll have to do better than that," said Martina.
"We need to get the whole bank involved so that all
the branches see it as their experiment, not just
Maplewood's."

"Perhaps we could have each branch select a
representative to observe the project and spread the
word about its success and failures," Andre said.

"I think that would help Maplewood too," Edmund
said. "It would give them a feeling of importance, that
the whole bank was watching."

"We need to make sure the observers know that
they're there to learn and help Western Security, not
play judge and jury in order to pronounce Maplewood
a failure," said Mike.

Dan was disconcerted by Mike's suggestion that he
might be seen as trying to upstage other managers and
branches. Mike had been diplomatic and had begun
with the positive, but Dan was still hurt—more than
he showed.

Dan saw himself as simply an ambitious person and
had dismissed suggestions that he was too aggressive as
the last whimpers of the dying breed of conservative
bankers. But the experiences at the managers' workshop had started him questioning his own style.
Although he didn't see himself as a competitive person
bent on succeeding at others' expense, he was beginning to realize that being seen as competitive was itself
a problem.

The department heads at Maplewood had nodded
agreement when Dan told them he was going to pro-

pose that Maplewood be a test site. But they were more outspoken when Dan reported back that he had received the go-ahead. They were nervous for similar reasons the steering committee had been: they worried that they and Dan would be suspected of trying to grab power. They had tried to keep Dan's head down. Now he was sticking it out.

Dan was expecting the department heads to be cautious about the project. But he was glad to see that they warmed up to the project as he answered their questions and revealed the plan.

The rest of the employees were enthusiastic when Dan introduced the purposes and processes of the customer service program at Maplewood. Though they had seldom discussed it, many employees felt that they were marginal to Western Security. They worried that the branch was in danger of being sold off or closed down because it had not acquired adequate market share.

The first step in implementing the program was to select a Maplewood customer team that would work with the Western Security steering committee. The committee was to be made up of one person from every department and level in the branch, and one person from each of the other branches.

After discussion with the steering committee, the branch team decided to have a one-day workshop focused on learning about the team organization model and thinking of specific ways the branch could improve its teamwork and customer service. "If it took the managers two days to catch on to the team organization model, employees should be able to figure it out in a day," quipped Beatrice, one of the branch team members.

In addition to readings on customer service, teamwork, and pull organization, the branch team distributed a summary of the conclusions the managers had reached at their workshop. Branch employees could incorporate the thoughts and hopes of others in the company as they began to plan.

Branch employees were cheerful and eager as they gathered for the workshop. They were excited about the first all-day meeting of the whole branch off-site. Being able to get together and talk was itself invigorating.

"We're fortunate to have Mark stop by and participate in the first part of the workshop with us," Beatrice began.

Mark gave a short background for the retreat, emphasizing his commitment to improving teamwork and customer service. "The executive team came to see how vital teamwork was to improving customer service and to winning and retaining the customers we need in order to survive and flourish. I'm surprised by how much we benefit from simply working on becoming a team organization. It gives me an extra shot of adrenalin in the morning—and it's not even caloric or habit-forming."

After Mark's talk, Beatrice had the employees form groups of three to discuss how teamwork to improve customer service could be useful for them and for Maplewood. The groups reported that teamwork for customer service would improve their pride in their jobs, help them develop interpersonal and banking skills, and give them credibility with other branches by contributing to their success.

The employees used the jigsaw method the managers had used to learn the team organization model. They formed five groups and each group was assigned the responsibility to learn one component. In new groups of five, they taught each other their parts. The groups also discussed how the components reinforced each other and critiqued the uses and limitations of the model.

"Now we want you to put your understanding of

teamwork to use by identifying major issues we should discuss and implement to improve how we work together to serve our customers," said Beatrice. "What can we do in the short term and long term to improve customer service and teamwork at Maplewood? We want practical solutions, of course, but also think in grand terms of where we should be headed." The groups of four were to brainstorm and then rank issues by priority.

Everyone discussed the groups' reports to get a consensus on major priority issues, and they narrowed it down to four. First, they needed a new way to direct flow so that customers would be greeted at the door and escorted to people who had the skills, authority, and availability to help them with their particular needs. They also needed to develop ways for employees to learn each other's jobs so that they could be more flexible. To help establish good relationships with customers and each other, employees could work on improving their interpersonal skills. Finally, the company needed to develop a compensation package compatible with the team approach, yet still oriented toward rewarding advanced skills, qualifications, and seniority.

"These are issues we can sink our teeth into," said Kenneth, another member of the branch customer team. He suggested that volunteers form task forces to accomplish their mission.

"The trouble is that everything is related to everything else," said an employee named Elizabeth. "What one task force recommends depends upon what others do."

"That's a good point," Kenneth said. "The branch team plans to coordinate the task forces. We want the task forces to cross-fertilize and share ideas, but it will be up to the branch team to ensure an integrated approach to change."

"So it's your team that's going to make decisions," said another employee.

"I guess you're suggesting that task forces might not have any real power . . ."

"It's a possibility," Elizabeth shrugged.

Beatrice stepped in and said, "Let me address the issue. We see ourselves as stimulating and coordinating and advocating, not telling and ordering. We know that we cannot succeed unless you succeed. If you think that we are being too pushy, tell us about it. Just remind us that you're using the team model to give us feedback and help us reflect!"

Once the task forces were formed they were asked to begin planning when and how they would continue their work over the next few weeks. The branch team recommended that the task forces be ready to make their recommendations in a month.

"On one hand, the day seems to have gone very fast, but on the other we seem to have accomplished a lot," said Kenneth. "Let's summarize the day by getting into groups of three to discuss how we want to work with each other, and what we want to avoid."

Ten minutes later, Kenneth asked the groups to report their ideas. The employees wanted to consult with and learn from each other, manage conflict, be available to help and support, and be upbeat. They wanted to avoid gossiping behind each other's backs, forming cliques, and assuming they had to compete to succeed.

Kenneth then asked them to talk briefly about what they personally got out of the workshop. Later they thanked each other for the day. One participant said, "We want to thank Beatrice, Kenneth, and others for taking the lead and giving us such good experiences today. I think I can speak for the group in saying that we have begun the journey and see the path into the future."

## Internal Service for External Service

Many customer service programs begin by training employees in human relations and teaching them technical skills. But frontline employees can dismiss such an approach as superficial. Often they feel they're being asked to do more without getting anything in return. They end up alienated and emotionally unprepared to serve customers with warmth and candor.

Developing better relationships within the company builds a stronger, more credible base for improving external service. The branch employees at Western Security felt like partners in an important joint enterprise, and could see how they, the company, and customers would benefit. They were prepared to reach out to customers, as their peers and bosses were reaching out to them.

## Value of Service Teams

Working together empowers employees. Serving customers well is a complex task that cannot be performed alone. Individuals need to pool their information, ideas, and assistance to solve customer problems. Employees benefit from talking to each other about how they can satisfy the complex needs of a client. When conflicts and mistrust develop, employees working together are more apt to find ways to reestablish a constructive relationship with the customer.

Many companies have successfully used teams to win and retain customers, especially in industrial marketing (Barrett, 1986; Bertrand, 1987). Several people working as a team can provide comprehensive service. They can analyze large customers' individual needs. By learning how these customers make their buying decisions, teams can create custom-tailored solutions and use marketing tools such as price discounts effectively. Sales teams make more productive sales calls, freeing the customer from repeating the same information to each salesperson with a different product line focus. A team is better equipped to establish a relationship that the customer sees as valuable, efficient, and considerate.

Teams are in a position to use special techniques and strategies to diagnose and improve the quality of service. Shostack (1984) and George and Gibson (1991) suggest, for example, blueprinting as a tool to manage service quality. The blueprint is a graphic illustration and flow chart showing the steps needed to deliver a service. A service delivery system may have evolved over years with additions being made, out of necessity, in a patchwork manner. The blueprint illustrates how service delivery connects a series of events to form an integrated whole that involves work both behind the scenes and in front of customers.

The blueprint can be used to identify possible "failpoints," processes most likely to go awry and compromise service. Through discussion centered on specific instances of failure, service team members can identify the most problematic steps in the process. The team can then rate the failpoints by priority and plan remedial action. By examining the service system as a whole, the team may also begin to invent a new delivery system.

With or without formal techniques such as blueprinting, the task of analyzing and strengthening service quality is a challenging one seldom brought about by speeches from management asking individuals to work harder. It takes team problem solving to find ways for everyone to work smarter.

### Structuring Service Teams

The team organization model provides a guide for forming service teams. Employees are inspired by a vision of becoming members of productive teams devoted to serving customers and each other. They are united in helping each other become more competent and effective. They empower each other by sharing their ideas and work. They explore the meaning of team organization and discuss problems in its implementation. They reflect on their progress in becoming a team that serves customers well.

Leaders like Mark and Dan need to work with and structure service teams. To do this, there are a number of strategies leaders can use, as outlined in the following list.

- *Show your support for teams to serve customers.* Leaders in talks, informal conversations, and newsletters describe their conviction that the company should work as a team. They publicly recognize concrete examples of team organization.
- *Negotiate a contract.* Employees explicitly state their commitment to attend and participate in the team meetings, work

to improve their skills and approaches, and help the team as a whole improve. This explicit contract is later used to help employees reflect on their teams.

- *Offer joint rewards.* The team as a whole is recognized in newsletters, has the opportunity to discuss its group's success to other employees who might be interested in service teams, and attends workshops and courses.
- *Offer individual rewards.* Members receive written recommendations that go into their individual files. Members are also complimented at performance appraisal for their contributions to the team.
- *Provide resources.* Employees will need flexibility to schedule convenient meeting times.
- *Strengthen support from leadership.* The leader attends some meetings, serves as an observer, asks for feedback and ideas, and inquires about the progress of the team.
- *Use "management by walking around" to "catch someone doing something right."* The leader drops in to observe the team in action, jots down notes to highlight something positive, and gives it to the team at an appropriate time.

Internal service reinforces external service; teamwork within the company is the foundation for constructive relationships with customers. Studies document that the teamwork model also applies to developing customer relationships. To serve customers well, frontline employees must communicate to customers that they share a common goal, that they want to encourage and empower them, and that they are willing to discuss conflicts openly and constructively. The next chapter looks at how this model can be used in working with customers.

8

# Working with Customers:
# The Bridge
# to Long-Term
# Relationships

*We think that good marketing is like a cable. We weave strands every day and finally we have a very strong link with our customers.*
                                                                —Joseph A. Lawton

"If knowing how to improve our skills in working with customers was easy, we wouldn't need a task force," Kenneth said with a laugh.

Kamil, an employee and member of the customer relationship task force, had just given a progress report to the branch team. The task force had begun enthusiastically and confidently, but eventually members felt frustrated and stymied. They had reached an agreement early on that employees should try to develop trusting relationships with customers, but then they got stuck. How could they teach these skills? What was different about how bank tellers and loan officers should operate?

"How about using the team organization model and the readings to help you be more specific," said Beatrice. "I read that research shows the basic ideas apply to working with customers as well as with employees."

"But how can that be?" Kamil asked. "How we act toward each other is so much different than with customers."

"But it's also the same, in ways," said Russ, another task force member. "Take trust, for instance. We want our colleagues to trust us, but certainly we want our customers to trust us too. I feel, in some sense, the same way about my regular customers as I do about my colleagues."

"I was talking to Catherine about this," Beatrice said. "She said we wanted team relationships up and down and around the organization, but how people put it into practice will vary. Employees want to be open with their bosses, for example, but the ways they choose to be open with them will be different than the ways they're open with a peer or someone who reports to them. The same logic applies to customers."

"I got some useful feedback from the branch team," said Kamil, introducing the next meeting of the customer relationship task force. "They wanted to remind us that we have a very challenging task and that they're not expecting quick success."

"I'm willing to give up on the quick part for the success part," said one of the members with a resigned laugh.

"They suggested that we use the team organization model," Kamil continued. "It's not as strange a notion as I first thought." He explained that how the model is put into practice is apt to vary a great deal depending on the situation.

"I like the idea that what you do depends upon the situation," Barbara, a task force member, said. "Some customers want small talk and others do not. As we decided before, we don't want to give people scripts that they are supposed to repeat. We want to give them choices."

"We're trying to empower our employees, not restrict them," agreed another member.

"Perhaps the model can be useful," Barbara said. "Let's go through the reading on team organization and brainstorm about how different parts of the model might apply."

After struggling to begin, they came to see that the vision part of the model had to do with the kind of relationship Maplewood wanted to have with customers. They wanted customers to trust them, rely on them, and talk to them about their interests and problems. They came to the conclusion that the team model should be part of their vision for working with customers.

"We want to offer effective, courteous, respectful service that customers find really valuable," Kamil summarized. "We're not talking about smiling more but not delivering the goods. Individual customers must leave believing we have given them what they need to get where they want to go. We must be credible."

As they discussed how to apply the idea of uniting, they decided that they wanted to convey to customers that the bank was on their side. Employees would need to communicate that customers' interests and goals were important. Speed of delivery was singled out as a very important goal because it showed that the bank considered customers' time valuable. Calling customers by name and getting to know them could also communicate cooperative goals.

The group had trouble thinking of reasons why customers might be interested in the bank's goals. Of course they wanted the customers to know that the bank and its employees were committed to serving them. But the more they talked, the more convinced they became that customers would feel more confident if they knew the bank's goals of developing loyal, long-term customers would make the branch a viable, secure investment for Western Security. Many customers were savvy enough to realize that the branch could only be a dependable partner in the long run if it was a successful business.

Employees also wanted to empower customers by showing them their patronage is valued. The bank wanted to show through investing in technology and other resources that it would continue to be able to meet customer expectations. The bank could provide forums such as interviews and focus groups so that customers could give feedback to the service providers.

"Interesting exercise," Barbara said. "But I'm not sure where we're going with this. What's our next step?"

"How about this," said Kamil. "We could get employees together and have them brainstorm about the kind of relationship they want to develop with customers. They could use the model and our ideas as beginning points."

"They could come up with some concrete guidelines and ideas about how they should act," Jo Ann said.

"Perhaps different groups could have their own discussions as well," said Barbara. "Loan people could talk about dealing with borrowers, tellers with people making quick transactions, and so on. They could come up with their own 'Do, Don't, and Maybe's.'"

"They could even train each other, practice, role-play—all sorts of things," Kamil said.

"We could take the roles of customers with different problems and attitudes, and then practice what we could do," Barbara said. "Others in the group could give feedback. This could get fun."

"I know," said Jo Ann, "We could make our own videos demonstrating some of the techniques and then show them to the rest of the branch and bank. We'll be movie stars!"

"The groups could also make proposals to managers about the authority they need to serve customers effectively," Kamil said.

"We should propose that these groups become ongoing," said Barbara. "People could get together every two weeks or so to reinforce the goal of serving customers and discuss specific issues."

"They could discuss an article, a new service, or a particular kind of customer," Jo Ann agreed.

"These groups could bring down all these ideas about serving customers to the practical, branch level," Kamil said. "They could talk about specific customers and give each other ideas and support. Employees would be learning and developing themselves at the same time."

The Maplewood team was delighted that the relationship task force had made progress. Kamil was concerned, though, that the mission of the relationship task force overlapped so much with the other task forces.

"But your ideas can help the other task forces," Russ said.

"Having employees discuss quality customer relationships and guidelines for developing them can help us implement the pull system and job flexibility program," Beatrice said.

Beatrice explained that the pull system task force had quickly confronted serious practical difficulties. Task force members realized that if greeting customers at the door and escorting them to the right person required much more labor, they would have difficulty getting it approved. They wanted to study carefully how cross-training people to do several jobs might increase labor efficiency and offset its costs.

The pull system task force also saw real risks. If Maplewood implemented the new system poorly, annoyed and inconvenienced customers might throw up their hands and look for another bank. It was always easier to lose a customer than to gain a new one. Although it might appear to be safer in the short run not to change, the task force concluded that not changing was probably more risky in the long run.

Implementing a pull system would not be a simple one- or two-step process, but an ongoing enterprise. Employees would need to reflect periodically on progress, make corrections, and plan how to improve.

The pull system task force wanted a slow, careful, continuous approach.

"We've been thinking about some kind of advertising," Russ said. "Do we want to get the word out that we're instituting new ideas to provide high-quality service to our customers? If so, how do we do it?"

"I have two immediate thoughts," Kamil said. "One is that we should be proud and advertise, and the second is that we don't want to promise more than we can do."

They agreed that the advertising had to be credible. Raising customer expectations and then not delivering could be disastrous. But advertising could further demonstrate to employees that Maplewood was serious. It might help orient customers so that they were not surprised and would be more understanding of the changes that Maplewood was making.

"In a way, advertising our intentions and abilities is another way of using the team organization model," Beatrice summarized. "It communicates to our customers what our vision is and how we're going to work with them to realize it."

## Value of Relational Marketing

Many companies have found that personal service is vital to business success (Sellers, 1990). A survey for the accounting and consulting firm Ernst & Young indicated that customers of banks and high-tech and manufacturing companies found "the personal touch"—as demonstrated by such things as how committed the company representative is to the client and whether he or she remembers the customer's name—to be more important than convenience, speed of delivery, or even how well the product works.

A survey by Opinion Research Corporation found that of four hundred executives of large companies the vast majority indicated that believing the airline cared about them was as important as prompt baggage delivery and efficient check-in. Burger

King used to rank speed of service first, but now ranks courtesy as the most important customer value. MasterCare found that their customers valued honest, courteous service twice as much as they valued low-cost auto repair.

Marketing researchers and specialists have urged companies to teach sales and service personnel to develop relationships with their customers (Jackson, 1985). More than just an exchange of money for goods, selling and service are functions of ongoing interpersonal relationships. Frontline employees who create strong relationships with customers build the foundation for repeat business (Spekman & Johnston, 1986; Soldow & Thomas, 1984).

Sales representatives and service personnel must be able to respond to customer inquiries and interests (Coppett & Staples, 1980; Weitz, Sujan, & Sujan, 1986). Oriented to individual customers, not just sales, they take the time to know their customers and adapt their approach to fit them (Michaels & Day, 1985). Relational marketing, in which the customer develops personal bonds with frontline employees, results in reliable repeat business (Dwyer, Schurr, & Oh, 1987).

Retaining customers is highly profitable for companies. Long-established customers typically buy more, refer more business, and are willing to pay higher prices. Moreover, getting new customers to replace lost ones is expensive. It may cost five times more to replace a customer than it costs to retain one (Hart, Heskett, & Sasser, 1990).

Relational marketing is also valuable to employees as people. Companies intent on building quality relationships with customers are also finding out their efforts contribute to employee morale; making customers happy makes employees happy (Sellers, 1990).

Taco Bell has asked its managers and employees to get to know their customers. Employees are to focus more on interacting with customers, and less on operations. Turnover among store managers has fallen from 50 percent to 20 percent, compared to the competition's 35 percent to 40 percent per year.

MBNA America, a credit card company, has used teamwork and customer service to hold on to 95 percent of its customers and to reduce turnover to 7 percent, one-third the industry average. Loyal customers are valuable to the company. A five-year customer contributes $100 a year to profits, but a ten-year customer contributes $300. In contrast, it costs the company $100 to acquire a new customer.

In its card retention department, phone service agents call every customer who wants to close an account and do whatever it takes, such as waive annual fees, to keep them. Their success rate is 50 percent. The collections department, which MBNA calls customer assistance, operates with the conviction that even long-delinquent customers "need a hugging, not a mugging." Over 95 percent of delinquent customers report that they find the collection agents polite.

The company rewards individuals and teams for quality service. When all groups achieve 97 percent of the performance standards on such dimensions as speed of answering inquiries, part of the company's profits goes into a bonus pool. The bonus pool is used to provide individual incentives, which can be as high as 20 percent of an employee's regular compensation.

MBNA America is in the enviable position of having twenty times more applicants than job openings. According to Senior Vice President Craig Smith, "it's much easier to work at a place where customers are happy . . . our commitment to keeping customers is the overriding reason why our employee turnover is low" (Sellers, 1990).

---

### Case Study: Banking with Chicago's South Side

South Shore Bank sits in the middle of the inner city of South Shore, fifteen minutes south of Chicago's Loop. Although 20 percent of the community's population lives on incomes below the poverty line, the bank's rate of loan failure is well below the national average (Grzywinski, 1991). Its secret of success: after years of neglecting local opportunities, the bank returned to the traditional principle of investing in and developing the community.

The management team that took over the bank in 1973 grew up on the idealism of John F. Kennedy, but was disenchanted with government programs that threw money at problems. They had joined with local forces and fought the sale of the bank to a group that wanted to move it downtown. With help from the federal and local governments and private investors, they raised the capital to buy the bank.

The bank's leaders were determined to reverse the spiral of community decline in which people stopped upgrading their homes, landlords stopped maintaining their apartment buildings, and store owners stopped improving their businesses and began moving them to other parts of Chicago. The former managers of the bank were telling people that the South Shore was a bad place to invest in. In its last two years, it made only two conventional home mortage loans for a total of $59,000.

The new managers realized that they needed their customers to participate in making the bank and the neighborhood a success. They had to work with community people to restore confidence.

The bank began with itself. It rearranged the entrance to make it more friendly, offered free parking, and opened a drive-in teller facility. Instead of red-lining the community and avoiding loans, loan officers had to defend why they wanted to turn down an applicant from the community. Top managers went to PTA meetings, block clubs, potluck dinners, and other neighborhood meetings to tell community members of the bank's aspirations and to listen to their needs.

Although originally focused on loans to small businesses, the bank found that residential development was the engine of change. The area had many large buildings, with thirty to forty units, but even more buildings with from six to twenty-four. But by 1970 the owners had decided that maintaining these units was too risky and had let them run down. Fortunately, the process had not continued to such a point that buildings could not be rehabilitated for quality, affordable housing.

The bank realized that it had to work with sub-neighborhoods, not just single buildings, to gain synergy. Investing in one building made investing in the next one less risky. Before giving a loan, the bank required the new owners to renovate. It favored owner occupancy so that owners would have a social as well as financial stake in the success of the building.

The bank attracted outside investment that spent nearly $8 million renovating 302 apartments in eleven buildings in a four-block area. When the first of thirty-six apartments became available, three hundred people signed up. Building on that success, the bank formed its own real estate development company to buy, renovate, and then operate or resell at a profit buildings adjacent to this project. The company's success, in turn, gave others confidence to invest.

The bank continued to work with outside private and government agencies to renovate whole areas. In addition, it worked with small housing entrepreneurs who bought and rehabilitated their own buildings without subsidies to take advantage of the new atmosphere of optimism and stability. The result was that four or five units of unsubsidized renovated housing were created for every unit of subsidized rehabilitated housing, a good deal for the community, the taxpayer, and the bank.

These entrepreneurs became invaluable partners. One entrepreneur, beginning with one housing project, eventually rehabilitated over fifty with the bank's help. Scores of people renovated one apartment, then bought a second, third, and fourth. These entrepreneurs networked to share skills, pass on secrets, and help each other squeeze a quarter's worth of rehabilitation out of a nickel. Yet they were still able to compete for tenants and prices.

South Shore Bank discovered that working with its customers requires sharing a common vision with the community, uniting behind the vision, empowering each other to be successful, exploring options, and creating solutions. Quality banking service is much more than quick smiles and snappy slogans. The challenges of establishing quality banking relationships are formidable for a bank like South Shore, but the rewards are rich.

---

## Complexities of Serving Customers

How should frontline employees work with and treat customers? What skills should they learn to improve their effectiveness? While there is general agreement upon the value of courtesy and friendliness, there are many different ideas about how to relate to customers. The often quoted slogan "the customer is always right" implies that employees should always be deferent and do what the customer demands. But there is also a common belief that effective salespeople take control of situations and establish dominance so that the customer eventually complies and makes the deal. Successful salespeople are thought to be aggressive and competitive.

Should marketing and service personnel be oriented to the customer or to the company? Frontline personnel represent the company's interests, yet also represent the customer to the company. Communicating a company orientation may alienate customers (Michaels & Day, 1985; Saxe & Weitz, 1982).

Working with customers can be complicated and difficult (Bowen & Lawler, 1992). Some training programs give frontline employees scripts and precise action plans to ensure a consistently high quality of service. Yet there are many situations that cannot be precisely predicted, and scripts cannot be developed for every possible circumstance. Nor is it likely that employees and customers appreciate a high level of uniformity, especially as customer needs become more specialized.

### Service Guidelines from the Team Organization Model

The team organization model is an important guide to relational marketing and working with customers because there is direct evidence that a track record of quality service is established through productive, cooperative relationships between frontline employees and customers (Tjosvold & Wong, 1991; Wong & Tjosvold, in press).

When a cooperative relationship has been established, customers believe they can rely on frontline employees and are open to being influenced. They feel the employee is on their side, will not mislead them, and will help them accomplish their goals. Employees who pursue their interests at the expense of the customer's, on the other hand, provoke mistrust. Customers become skeptical and are reluctant to cooperate.

The team model helps to settle the debate about whether service providers and salespeople should be oriented to the customer or to the company. Frontline employees are ambassadors who work to promote the mutual interests of the company and customer. Of course, company and customer interests are not completely compatible. However, employees can help customers see specific issues, such as price, within a larger cooperative context and recognize the value of negotiating for mutual benefit.

Frontline employees who act as though they're placing customers' interests before the company's are likely to be considered disingenuous. Most consumers are worldly enough to know that companies pay employees to sell their products. Customers are also likely to suspect employees who seem indifferent to customers' interests. Developing a cooperative relationship committed to mutual benefit is a practical approach to the demands of selling to customers and serving them.

The team organization model also guides sales and service people in developing the skills and sensitivities they need to serve employees well. It provides direction and clarifies ambiguities, but it is not a straitjacket dictating one specific way to treat customers. Frontline employees use their knowledge about teamwork and their experiences working together to develop ways of forming relationships that fit themselves and their customers. They can brainstorm about possible scenarios, practice managing them, give each other feedback, and reflect on their experiences.

## Ways of Learning Together

Serving customers involves developing relationships in which customers find real value so that they become committed to continued patronage. Employees must also develop open, productive relationships with each other. They must help each other refine their capabilities and apply their learning to build strong, trusting relationships with customers and between themselves.

In service teams and in specially created learning teams, employees give each other the courage and savvy to become effective and competent colleagues and service providers. They meet regularly to talk about ways of strengthening their teamwork skills (Johnson & Johnson, 1989b; Tjosvold & Tjosvold, 1991). Teams function as informal support groups, allowing employees to share problems and let off steam, and enabling more experienced employees to serve as mentors and assistants, fostering camaraderie and shared success. Service and learning teams are safe places where members experience caring, laughter, and support for their determination to work as a team to serve customers.

Employees use their service and learning teams for professional discussions in which they can talk honestly about their challenges, frustrations, and opportunities. They discuss, in concrete and precise terms, the ways that customer service and team organization can be applied. Through discussing, explaining, and teaching, they deepen their understanding and expand their skills in customer service and teamwork.

Together, employees plan programs and activities designed to strengthen their abilities. They share the burden and excitement of developing abilities and learning from each other's experience. As each becomes more able, they help others be more effective. As the more experienced employee teaches the less experienced, the more experienced employee learns, too.

Most employees are unsure of how they affect customers and each other. Thus, it's helpful if they can observe each other serving customers and give each other feedback. They can discuss strengths and weaknesses and plan how they can help each other improve. Observation and feedback should be reciprocal to emphasize that everyone has something to learn — and teach. Of course, employees need to be respectful and, when pointing out shortcomings, recognize that everyone has strengths and weaknesses and good and bad days.

Creating service teams focused on learning and forming actual learning teams are initiatives that demonstrate a company's commitment to increasing its employees' competence and well-being. One of the most compelling reasons for instituting team organization is that it promotes people. Everyone wins when people learn.

Developing cooperative relationships with customers and with colleagues requires that employees deepen their sensitivities and strengthen their skills in working with others. The most difficult intricacies of cooperative work involve coping with problems and frustrations. The next part examines how employees can manage conflict and anger to strengthen the bonds between themselves and customers.

# Part Four

# REFINING
# ABILITIES

*The person who grabs the cat by the tail learns about 44 percent faster than the one just watching.*

—Mark Twain

Conflict, and the anger and frustration that accompany it, pose particular challenges to cooperative work. But conflict and anger can also strengthen interpersonal skills, and managing them constructively can stimulate spirited employee teamwork and solid customer relationships. However, confusion and ambiguity often make learning more difficult. Therefore, skillful reflection is often needed to enhance employees' interpersonal sensitivities and enable them to be more effective colleagues and service providers as well as family and community members.

# 9

# Managing Conflicts:
# Continuous Problem Solving
# Between Customers and Teams

*I dogmatize and am contradicted, and in this conflict of opinions and sentiments I find delight.*

—Samuel Johnson

"Then he leans forward with a fake smile and says, 'I'm the secretary of the local business chamber, and when I talk about how difficult it is to work with this bank at the next meeting, you, your boss, and your customer service program won't look good,'" said Jackie. "Then he just sat back and smirked. I got really flustered. I was so hurt, embarrassed, and angry I didn't know what to say."

Jackie, a loan officer at the Maplewood branch, had been telling her service team about her latest meeting with Roger Donahue. Roger was the self-described upcoming boy wonder of the local business community. He had managed to convince a major cellular telephone company that it needed an aggressive salesperson like him to be its local agent. Roger had spent lavishly on hiring other aggressive salespeople and renting fancy office space: he even purchased his own hot-air balloon to advertise himself and his agency.

123

Predictably enough, he faced a cash flow problem. It took him a while to realize that selling cellular phones was not the high-tech pathway to an instant fortune: it was another highly competitive industry in which controlling costs was critical. Jackie had her suspicions that he was spending unwisely reaffirmed when she looked over his quarterly profit and loss statement that the loan terms required he send her. She asked him to meet with her to discuss the business, generally, and his loan, specifically. Jackie had hoped to show that she and the bank were on his side and wanted him to succeed but thought it would be best to talk about problems sooner rather than later. She was worried when she had to call him several times before pinning him down to a meeting time.

Unfortunately, Roger was defiant. He labeled Jackie's expression of concern as unnecessary meddling. He angrily declared that, as a dynamic young entrepreneur, he would soon have considerable financial leverage, beyond the bank's control. Once he had achieved his success, he would remember his friends and his enemies.

"Tell him to stuff it," said Brent, a fellow loan officer. "These ideas about serving our valued customers are all right, in general, but when you get guys like this, who needs 'em. Pull the plug on the loan — let him sink."

"That's a little drastic, isn't it?" said Sabrena, another colleague of Jackie's. "We're supposed to be working with our customers. He does have profile in the community and he could hurt us. And if we call the loan now we may not get much of it back."

"He's a spoiled, egocentric brat. We don't need him, and we'll be doing the community a favor letting him crash," Brent said. Sensing that Jackie was taken aback, he continued, "Don't get me wrong, I'm angry with Roger, not you or Sabrena."

"I need direction," Jackie said. "I think I should try

to help him, but I sort of feel like Brent. Why should I bang my head against the wall for this guy?"

"Didn't we read somewhere in the team organization literature about how it was necessary to manage our conflicts?" Thomas said. He was now a teller on the same service team as Brent and Jackie. He sympathized with their frustration.

"I remember that," Sabrena said. "I'd never come across the idea that we could manage conflict before. I thought conflict did the controlling, and the best you could do was to stay out of its way as much as possible."

"I liked that part of the model the best," Brent said. "I like showing conflict who's boss."

"We noticed," Sabrena teased.

"But I just assumed that we were to manage our conflicts with each other; it's a little hard to see how we can manage our conflicts with customers," said Brent.

"Even with customers we're supposed to manage our conflicts," Thomas said. "But what's frustrating is, even if we communicate to the customer that we're on their side and want to help them, not everything will go smoothly."

"I couldn't get Roger to believe I was on his side," Jackie said.

"You had a lot of help from Roger," Brent said. "People like that don't want to believe. They think, 'If you don't agree with me and do what I want, then you're against me pure and simple.'"

"Well put," Sabrena said. "How can we communicate to customers that we are on their side even when we disagree with them? It's not just Roger who gets confused. I do too!"

"What's that old saying?" Jackie mused. "'Love me, love my dog.' If you don't love my dog, then you obviously don't love me."

"In Roger's defense, he's got everything invested in

his business," Sabrena said. "His ego, his reputation, his house; it's not always easy to face up to reality."

"He's not the only borrower who ever found himself sinking into a quagmire," Jackie said.

"That's for sure," said Thomas. "Even respectable, stable types can go crazy when bad things happen to their business. All hell breaks loose."

"Not only is the customer not always right, sometimes they are very wrong," Brent said. "We cannot just tell them we're on their side. We have to get our money back, not give them more."

"But don't you think if we really have good relationships with our customers, then we won't have so many problems?" said Jackie.

"If Roger was a more open person, perhaps he could see that you were on his side, and that would have made it much easier for you to talk to him and do business," Brent said. "But you would still have had problems to discuss."

"We have conflicts with people on the bank floor, too," Thomas said. "I've had customers ask me to forgive charges because they meant to deposit their money earlier. Once somebody asked me to give them $40,000 cash on the spot. All sorts of things like that happen. Perhaps they're more minor than you get in loans, but they happen all the time!"

"Let's face it, some of these valued customers are just unreasonable in their demands," Brent said.

"The customer is not always right, but we can't fight with them and tell them they're wrong," Jackie said. "I don't see where fighting will pay off."

"We need a relationship in which we can talk about problems and difficulties," Thomas said. "Sort of like what we're doing now."

"Sort of is right," Sabrena said. "I can't see having this kind of discussion with customers."

"The model tells us to find ways to explore and discuss different ideas for solving problems," Jackie said. "That's not easy to do with customers, but it is necessary."

"I remember one conflict that we worked out well," Thomas said. "You know that soft-spoken, elderly woman who handles about twenty-six different banking accounts, Mrs. Swanson? She works with group homes for mentally handicapped people, and she's in charge of the residents' money. Now it's good public relations and just good for us to have their business, but of course we don't make any money on it—lots of transactions but no more than two hundred dollars in the biggest account.

"The trouble was that she got in the habit of coming here on Friday nights and using the drive-up teller. It would make us nuts because we knew that people waiting behind her were wondering what was taking us so long. So Jackie and I decided to talk to her about her banking needs and her job, tell her we were glad to help, and ask her if she could come into the bank on some day other than Friday. After our talk, we knew her better and she knew us better, and we all left happy."

"Mrs. Swanson is not the same kind of person as Roger," Sabrena said.

"Definitely not," Thomas agreed.

"But still, it makes me think that if we put our heads together, perhaps we can come up with a plan for approaching Roger," said Jackie. "There must be some way that we can show him we are not out to get him, but that we must protect the bank's interest."

"We're going to have to be creative and disciplined at the same time," Brent said. "We can't let ourselves get sidetracked."

"We also have to realize that we may not succeed," said Thomas. "He's got to respond. We can pitch him the ball, but he's got to hit it."

"If he doesn't respond well, we still want to leave the table feeling that we gave him a good chance and didn't act hastily," Jackie said.

"We should remember that even if he remains defiant and defensive, there's a chance that someday he might think about what we've told him," Sabrena said.

"Yes, we can defend our interests, just so long as we don't get defiant and defensive ourselves," Thomas said.

"Just talking like this has made me feel much better about talking to Roger again," Jackie said. "I guess I understand now what it means to manage our conflicts together."

## Conflict and Customers

To serve customers is to be in conflict with them. Service providers and salespeople act as liaisons between the company and its customers. Inevitably, companies will have expectations, perspectives, positions, and interests that conflict with their customers', requiring them to develop negotiation skills (Perdue, Day, & Michaels, 1986; Swartz & Brown, 1991).

Perfect harmony is an unrealistic goal for working with customers. It leads people to assume that they should avoid conflicts or smooth them over. But it is the skilled management of conflict that builds effective customer relationships (Swartz & Brown, 1991). At times, avoiding and smoothing over are appropriate, but important issues with valued customers call for direct, open discussions to resolve issues for mutual benefit.

Conflicts involve incompatible activities: what one person is doing is interfering, frustrating, or in some other way making another's actions less effective (Deutsch, 1973). Not all conflicts arise from opposing goals and interests. A counselor and client may both be working to increase the client's happiness and effectiveness, but the client may believe the counselor should solve a problem, and the counselor may believe the client should.

What is critical for resolving conflicts, many studies show, is that people develop an understanding of and trust in their shared goals through open discussion of the issues (Deutsch, 1973, 1980, 1990; Tjosvold, 1985a). They need to believe that, though they disagree, they do not want to gain at the other's expense. Thus, they do not let the conflict degenerate into a battle in which the victor takes all. They use the conflict to understand each other and the issue better, explore different points of view, combine ideas to create solutions, and reach agreements that further their common objectives.

A borrower and a loan officer share the goal of administering a loan so that it works for the borrower and the bank. The borrower uses the loan to build a business, believing the business will earn enough to repay the loan with interest. Feeling grateful for the assistance, the borrower wants to do business with the bank again. The borrower also wants the bank to feel secure about its loan and not have thoughts about recalling it; in the long term, the borrower wants the bank to prosper so it can continue to be an ally. However, the loan officer and lender are apt to disagree about the terms of the contract that will allow the bank to feel secure and the borrower to feel assisted. The loan officer needs to work with the customer to develop terms that they both find fair and useful.

## Cooperative Conflict Management

Conflicts need not threaten relationships between employees and customers. The failure to discuss conflicts in an open and constructive way, however, can pose a serious threat. Surveys indicate that only four customers out of one hundred register complaints with a company, but customers who do register complaints are actually more likely to remain loyal than those who do not (Zemke & Schaaf, 1989). The greatest danger is for customers to feel frustrated and walk away, because they will end up giving their business to the competition.

### Open Discussion

By bringing up problems, customers give the company an opportunity to address shortcomings and demonstrate its commitment to high-quality customer service. The company can make amends and use the customer's ideas to solve problems. Indeed, customer feedback can fuel the innovation and change needed to stay competitive in today's market.

Open discussion of problems is also critical for managing the internal dynamics of a team and organization (Johnson, Johnson, Smith, & Tjosvold, 1990; Maier, 1970; Tjosvold, 1991a). Through the clash of opposing views, employees can dig into issues, recognize the shortcomings of their present approaches, and create vital new solutions.

Open discussion requires a great deal. People have to be willing to discuss their positions and the ideas and logic that support them. They must also be open-minded and consider different perspectives. They must grapple with new information and alter their thinking.

### Moving Beyond Avoidance

Every day many customers conclude that it is not worth the effort to make their concerns and complaints public. They take the most expedient route and either resign themselves to inferior service or find an alternative.

Avoiding open conflict is a pervasive tendency within organizations (Cosier & Schwenk, 1990). Employees avoid discussing their views and frustrations directly with their co-workers and continue to work in unproductive ways. Managers consider it prudent to feign agreement, withhold information, and let inadequate decisions go unchallenged. They try hard to be upbeat and optimistic. They want to "cooperate" and "support" each other. They don't want to rock the boat or upset the team, and they don't want to risk asking embarrassing questions or saying something that is "wrong." Head nodding and smiles are easy ways to avoid conflict. Silence often gives the illusion of agreement.

Perhaps the overriding reason that so many people expend so much effort avoiding open discussion of problems is the false assumption that conflict is inevitably disruptive and destructive. In addition, the risks of discussing differences openly are immediate and tangible whereas the value of controversy for increased productivity and happier people seems more distant.

Not understanding how to make controversy productive, many people are too inhibited to make a stand.

Avoiding conflict does not solve problems or dissolve opposing perspectives. The customer may say the service is fine yet decide never to go to that restaurant again. People may pay lip service to a group's decision, but grumble and gossip in private. They may engage in a variety of political actions to influence decisions indirectly. They may form coalitions of similar-minded people and wage quiet warfare. The coalitions help them resist the majority, spread rumors discrediting the current policy, and plot ways to elevate one of their own to leadership. It is unlikely that this political infighting is organizationally useful (Eisenhardt, 1989; Eisenhardt & Bourgeois, 1988).

Employees often assume that a customer's complaint or an employee's question is a sign of failure. They make the unrealistic assumption that a problem-free relationship is both desirable and possible. Yet problems and conflicts are inevitable, and potentially highly constructive. Problems and conflicts are signs that people depend upon each other, giving them the opportunity to reflect on how their relationship can be improved. They can use problems to learn more about themselves and about others.

### Mutual Benefit

Open discussion needs to be infused with the clear intent to solve the problem in a way that gives mutual benefit (Deutsch, 1990; Tjosvold, 1989a). Employees must communicate to customers that they want a solution that works for the customer and for the company. Within an organization, employees must strive for solutions that help both people and departments reach their goals. They must avoid giving the impression that they are only watching out for themselves or that they want to win at others' expense. Undertaken with a spirit of mutual understanding, the open discussion of problems results in high-quality solutions that leave both sides committed to their relationship. Employees have the right to disagree, but they have the corresponding responsibility to develop strong, cooperative relationships in which they can disagree in a productive manner (Tjosvold, 1991c) (see Figure 9.1).

Figure 9.1. Dynamics of Managing Conflict Cooperatively.

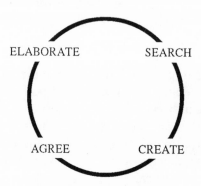

## Dynamics of Managing Conflict Cooperatively

Managing conflicts productively requires persistence, skill, and ingenuity. When discussed openly for mutual benefit, problem-solving discussions explore issues in depth, encourage people to elaborate their views, create options, and integrate apparently opposing positions (Johnson & Johnson, 1987; Pruitt, 1981; Tjosvold, 1985a, 1991a). In this way, the participants are prepared for future collaboration and conflict management.

### Elaborate Positions and Interests

Cooperative conflict management begins when at least one person directly communicates that there is a conflict that needs to be discussed and resolved for mutual benefit. The involved parties sit down and clarify and define the conflict. Each side describes the other's actions and explains why the other's behavior is interfering with or frustrating them. Rather than blame and evaluate, they share their perceptions and feelings. They recognize that people cannot read minds, but need direct information about each other's feelings and beliefs. Rather than seeing the conflict as a win-lose struggle, they define it as a mutual problem to be solved. No one loses when people solve a mutual problem.

Participants listen to learn more about each other's needs,

interests, and feelings. Then they elaborate on how their proposals can meet the needs of all parties. They critique others' proposals and point out inadequacies. However, they remain willing to change their position when persuaded of another proposal's superiority.

It is critical that employees focus on needs and goals, not positions. Cooperative negotiators refuse to compromise their own or others' interests, but they are flexible when it comes to constructing a solution that will be most beneficial for all. Successful proposals are those that meet the needs of all parties.

Effective negotiators do not assume that, because opposing positions and proposals are incompatible, the parties' basic goals and interests are. They seek solutions that further the needs of all parties so that everyone is committed to resolving the conflict. They see that they have more to gain by negotiating a settlement than by continuing a conflict.

### Search for and Demonstrate Understanding

One of the advantages of conflict is that it allows individuals to learn about others' unique perspectives and realize how they are different from and similar to their own. To come to a mutually beneficial agreement, negotiators have to understand and accurately assess others' perspectives.

There are many obstacles to this understanding. People can misinterpret another's motivation and emotional intensity. They can exaggerate or discount their differences or similarities. Moreover, people in conflict often feel they are not understood and repeat their arguments in ever stronger and louder terms. They become intransigent or give up convinced that the other party is not listening and reconciliation is impossible.

To avoid this standoff, it is often helpful for each party to present the other's position. This shows that they are trying to understand each other and gives the opposing party a chance to correct any misperceptions that are revealed. When both parties stop repeating arguments and start listening to other views, they are in a better position to come to a resolution.

## Create Integrated Options

The obstacles to creating solutions are formidable. Perhaps the most common one is fixating on an original proposal as if that were the only one that could satisfy a given party's requirements. Rigidly committing to their own position, people have a tendency to define the issue in terms of "our way or their way."

Similarly, there is a tendency to assume a fixed pie: the more one gets, the less the other gets. This is often accompanied by a short-term perspective. However, there's almost always enough "pie" to go around, especially in the long term. A manufacturer and a supplier have opposing interests regarding the price of supplies, but both will benefit from a stronger relationship that enables them to reduce costs, improve quality, and increase profitability. Generally, the more one gets, the more the other gets.

Premature evaluation can also get in the way of creating alternatives. Some people are so prepared to pounce on the drawbacks of any new idea that they discourage others from proposing ideas.

To overcome these obstacles and create alternatives, opposing parties should brainstorm and invent as many options as they can. The more ideas, the more likely it is that a good one can be selected. Later, people can evaluate ideas on the extent to which they promote mutual benefit.

Negotiators can bundle ideas together and propose package deals. Thus, they can reach agreement on several issues simultaneously and everyone can see that their interests have been protected and promoted on at least some of the issues. Similarly, people can reach agreement on different issues in which a settlement on one issue is linked to a settlement on another.

## Reach an Agreement

Effective agreements satisfy both sides' legitimate interests and reconcile opposing needs. But no matter how elegant the solution, it is not going to solve the conflict unless all parties are committed to implementing it. The agreement should help people put the conflict behind them and prepare for future collaboration. Proceeding successfully through the prior steps is critical for arriving at these agreements.

Typically, conflicts should be resolved on the basis of objective criteria (Fisher & Ury, 1981). Proposals should be evaluated according to standards of fairness, efficiency, community values, and scientific merit. Together, people should decide which standards are most important, evaluate the options, and make a decision based on the standard they value most. When such an approach is not possible, people can resort to other methods, such as taking turns, drawing lots, or letting someone else decide.

Agreements should announce the conflict's resolution, describe how people are to behave in the future, stipulate what should happen if people fail to live up to the agreement, and identify times to discuss whether additional steps are needed to improve the relationship. Everyone should be prepared to open up negotiations if the solution proves ineffective. They should remember that success in negotiations comes when all parties get what they really want, to the extent that it is possible.

### Reflect and Learn

After the conflict has been resolved, people can reflect back on their negotiations to learn more about how they and how others manage conflict. Discarding mistaken ideas that they should be able to manage conflict perfectly, they can seek to deepen their sensitivities and improve their abilities. They can give and receive feedback and support each other's efforts to change. Together they can celebrate their success and overcome failure. They can see how learning to manage conflict actually binds them together in a dynamic cycle of cooperative activities.

### Consequences

Constructive conflict has been shown to give rise to high-quality, innovative solutions and agreements. The mix and clash of ideas bring to light new positions not previously considered. These positions often combine several people's arguments and perspectives in elegant ways.

When conflicts are managed cooperatively, people feel satisfied knowing they have benefited from the discussion. They feel inspired by the challenge and develop positive attitudes toward the experience. They remain committed to the new agreement because they know their own interests have been represented and understand the reasoning behind the solution. Controversy, then, is critical for successful conflict management and a shared commitment (Tjosvold, 1987).

The rewards of successful conflict management are rich indeed. When cooperative goals are emphasized, conflict stimulates people intellectually and emotionally and results in effective solutions, high morale, and strengthened relationships.

---

### Special Focus: Managing Environmental Conflicts

Environmentalism may well be the most potent worldwide movement in the 1990s and one to which businesses and organizations will have to respond (Kirkpatrick, 1990). Liberal and conservative, old and young, people from developed and developing nations are worried about the damage done to air, water, and land. Mutual fund companies advertise that they only invest in companies with strong environmental records. Stores have gained market share by featuring environment-friendly products.

Wise managers are recognizing that demonstrating concern for the environment is good business. They fear the risk of facing increasingly costly regulation and consumer backlash. They want to avoid Exxon's plight. After the oil spill in Alaska, 41 percent of Americans seriously considered boycotting the company.

Edgar Woolard, CEO of Du Pont, has called environmental problems the single most important issue for industry to address. Du Pont has committed itself to finding safe alternatives to chlorofluorocarbons (CFCs) – a $750 million-per-year business in which it is the industry leader – by the year 2000. Although the company could try to delay, because CFCs are not a proven hazard, it recognizes that it must deal with the probability that they are.

Managing conflict directly and cooperatively is a credible way to be part of the environmental solution, not the problem. Instead of resisting environmental groups and responding only under coercion, progressive companies are involving environmentalists in their decision making.

Pacific Gas and Electric Company (PG&E) learned from conflicts in the 1970s, in which environmental groups successfully blocked the building of several giant coal and nuclear power plants. PG&E decided that it had benefited from discussions with environmental groups and now aggressively seeks dialogue with them. Internal environmentalists are encouraged to press their concerns and ideas to shape company policy. Melvin Land, a well-known West Coast environmentalist, now sits on the board of PG&E.

PG&E's CEO, Richard Clark, advises that environmental considerations should be an integral part of any decision the company makes, not something extra thrown in the pot. PG&E seeks a continuing relationship with environmental groups, even those that opposed the company in the past. It has undertaken a $10 million study with the Natural Resources Defense Council on how to generate electricity in a more energy-efficient manner.

Environmentalism is not an issue that will be solved or go away. It requires ongoing dialogue and conflict management. As knowledge develops, attitudes and solutions will change. In the mid 1970s, McDonald's changed from paper to plastic packaging because of customers' concerns about cutting trees and the high energy consumption of paper production. It has made major efforts to reduce waste, recycle what is used, and explain what it is doing. Scientists now have convinced company environmentalists that plastic is more recyclable and less damaging to the environment. McDonald's is now trying to explain to customers the advantages of plastic for protecting the environment (Kirkpatrick, 1990).

---

## Approaching Customers

Managing conflict requires openness, discipline, and creativity. Especially when working with customers, employees have to be as prudent and restrained as they are open and expressive. Showing respect for other people and not blaming them enables people to work for mutual benefit. Most customers are not prepared to be blamed or criticized by a service provider. Customers may not always be right, but they are seldom prepared to accept that they are wrong.

There is no magical phrase or simple procedure for managing conflict, and discussing conflicts with customers requires particular sensitivity and discipline. Employees can use service and learning teams to discuss written materials, practice techniques, and reflect on their experiences in order to refine and strengthen the complex skills required for conflict management (Tjosvold, 1989b, 1991a). The next chapter gives guidelines for managing the intense feelings sometimes aroused by conflict.

# 10

# Managing Frustration
# and Anger:
# Key Skills
# for Effective Teamwork

*Have you learned lessons only of those who admired you, and were tender with
you, and stood aside for you?*
*Have you not learned great lessons from those who braced themselves against
you, and disputed the passage with you?*

*—Walt Whitman*

"I guess we can scratch 'The customer is always
right' from first place in our guidelines for customer
relationships," Kamil said with feigned seriousness.

Kamil, Jo Ann, and others on the customer relationship task force had invited Jackie to give them a
firsthand report on her service team. She had described
how her team had helped her gain some perspective
and create and carry out a plan for dealing with
Roger.

"Sounds like your plan was a good one, if not
completely successful," said Barbara.

"You can't win them all," Jackie replied. "But we're
satisfied we did what we could and acted responsibly
and competently. We know we can't control him. It's
his life and he's got to make his own decisions. I hope
for him as well as for us that he makes some good
ones."

**139**

"I like it that you didn't get into the tit-for-tat game," Jo Ann said.

"It's so easy to get into that kind of squabbling," Barbara said. "You showed real discipline. I admire that."

"We weren't so disciplined afterwards," Jackie said. "Thomas and I went to the racket courts talking, yelling, and ventilating. Had a great game and got back to the office in good enough shape to get some work done."

"Sounds fun," Jo Ann smiled. "Roger might even learn. Maybe not this year or even next year, but someday he'll wake up and realize that he can't just push people around. He might even remember that the bank helped him. Stranger things have happened."

"Jackie's story makes it obvious that we have to discuss problems and conflicts with customers," Jo Ann said.

Calling upon their own experiences and the team organization model, Jackie and the task force brainstormed about ways Maplewood's employees could discuss problems with customers. They saw that it was vital for employees to have the skills and know the procedures for discussing issues openly and cooperatively. Employees represented the bank's interests in serving customers well, but they also had to protect the bank's credibility and profitability. It would not be easy.

"We have to revise our thinking a little bit," said Barbara. "We've been focused on the happy, upbeat part of working with customers: how we needed to celebrate our achievements and keep everyone happy about serving customers."

"That seems a little narrow now," Jo Ann said. "Employees have lots of frustration and anger to deal with."

"It's true," Barbara said. "You can't expect to have a relationship with an employee, a spouse, or anyone that is all sweetness and caring. Even Hollywood doesn't pretend 'they lived happily ever after' anymore."

"It's also a two-way street," Jackie said. "Customers get frustrated and angry with us; we get angry and stressed with them."

"But what do we know about anger and frustration?" Jo Ann asked. "It's easy to see the value of celebrating successes and talking about mistakes and frustrations. But I don't think managing our anger and stress is something we all know about. It seems like we should do some reading and thinking, and maybe even talk to some people who study it."

"I agree there's always more to learn, but I've been managing anger and frustration for almost fifty-five years," said Barbara. "I remember reading someplace about not letting anyone 'push your button.' That idea has been very useful to me."

"You've got to stay cool under pressure, but that's tough to do," Jo Ann said.

"It's not always a matter of just being cool," Barbara said. "Sometimes you feel angry and need to express it, but you should stay in control of your own feelings. You don't want others to be in control."

"You're talking as if getting angry was a very rational process," Jo Ann said. "I don't decide to get angry, I just do, even when I don't want to."

"I'm not sure how it works, but I know I can control it somewhat," Barbara said.

"We can control what we do and say, certainly, at least most of the time," Kamil said. "We're getting back to the idea of choices again. We need to let employees know what their choices are and how they can make them."

"We don't want people to do whatever comes naturally, without thinking," Jackie said.

"Yes, I agree. I've learned that it's better to avoid taking the approach that 'I'm right, you're wrong,'"

Barbara said. "People don't like being attacked and told they're wrong."

"But when someone's angry with you, it's because they blame you and think you're wrong," said Jo Ann.

"I guess it's how strong you come across," Barbara said. "Most people will admit to making mistakes, but they don't want to be accused of acting deliberately to harm you."

"You mean go easy," Kamil suggested.

"Not always. With a guy like Roger you need to be direct, just not accusatory," Barbara replied.

"Self-righteousness won't get you very far with a guy like Roger," said Jackie.

"Nor with most people," Kamil added.

"It's difficult finding the right way of expressing anger toward each other, much less toward customers," Jo Ann said.

Barbara nodded in agreement. "It would be disastrous if everyone decided to let it all hang out."

"Is there some way we can all continue thinking about this?" asked Kamil.

"Our service group is looking for readings and training," Jackie said. "We think they'll help us learn more about dealing with conflict and the anger and frustration that go with it."

### Putting Anger to Work

The Maplewood task force was confronting the assumption that anger is necessarily so disruptive that it should be avoided. Anger is commonly thought to signify immaturity and a lack of personal control. A manager's angry outburst fuels suspicion and mistrust. It undermines the image of an outgoing, approachable person or a firm-handed, respected disciplinarian. Angry employees are fired; extremely angry people are locked up in prisons and institutions.

Traditional organizations teach employees to suppress anger. Organizations have been thought of as "machines" in which people are supposed to be "businesslike" and devoid of feelings. However, modern companies are trying to promote shared values and a common mission to serve their customers well. They believe employees should have bosses and colleagues who care about them, listen to their feelings, and provide a sense of support and caring that enhances their self-esteem.

The emphasis on "upbeat, positive" values and feelings often leaves little place for anger. But anger will not be shoved aside or driven away. It affects individual well-being and customer service, whether people want it to or not.

The stereotypes of anger are destructive; anger itself is not. When anger is driven underground, people do not learn to understand it or manage it constructively (Tjosvold, Tjosvold, & Tjosvold, 1991). Employees need knowledge and skill to make reasonable choices about how they should handle their anger and respond to customers' anger.

## Identifying the Causes of Anger

People often talk about becoming angry as if the cause were external to themselves. "He made me angry!" "It just came over me!" But people decide whether they will get angry, how much they will get angry, and how they will express it. Unfortunately, most people are not aware of making these decisions and make them so quickly that they feel controlled by their anger. They report that they are unable to stop themselves from getting angry and losing control. Yet we control anger, anger does not control us. Unfortunately, many people are unaware of how they choose to be angry.

Anger is more than frustration. We get angry when we hold another responsible for our frustration, and believe that the person could have avoided interfering with our efforts (Averill, 1982). Anger is based on the belief that someone has caused us avoidable, unjustified frustration. The offending party is thought to have done the misdeed deliberately and with no compensating rationale. People who obstruct us with sufficient reason or without intention or knowledge may annoy but not anger us. We get angry when a colleague leaves us extra work because he wants to lie on the beach, but not when he has to attend a sick child. Anger appears to be particularly strong when others are thought to be sabotaging our self-esteem and social status.

Anger involves how people think about and experience a conflict. Jackie could get angry when Roger blames her for his difficulties in meeting the loan payments. She could hold him responsible for an unnecessary, insulting attack. She could get even angrier if she dwelt on the work she had done on his behalf and the trust she had shown in giving Roger the loan to begin his business.

But Jackie does not have to be angry. With another perspective, she can react much differently to Roger's outburst. If she considered the possibility that Roger was under tremendous stress and unable to control his feelings, she could see the outburst as a sign of his own turmoil. She would be even less frustrated if she thought Roger felt guilty about attacking her or if he made a genuine apology and thanked her for not bearing a grudge against him.

We decide how we are going to experience a frustration, and that, in turn, affects our feelings. Then we decide how we are going to act on these feelings. Because we have such power does not mean that we should work to avoid or minimize anger, for sometimes feeling and expressing anger can be very constructive.

### The Positive Side of Anger

Contrary to popular belief, anger is not an antisocial force. People who were asked to keep detailed diaries of their anger and irritation were found to get angry with other people, seldom with inanimate objects (Averill, 1982). Most often they got angry with loved ones and people they liked, and sometimes with acquaintances. The least likely target of anger was someone they didn't like.

Anger, managed openly and skillfully, contributes significantly to relationships and teamwork. It sets in motion a process that can help a group reexamine its mission, emphasize team members' interdependence, reaffirm people's power, and focus attention on relationships that need strengthening. While anger is often managed destructively, it has a vital function in ensuring productive teamwork.

Anger mobilizes people and increases the vigor of their actions. People can use this energy to deal with problems and achieve their goals. Anger also transforms internal anxiety to external conflict. It can help people overcome their fears and inhibitions so they can take action, defend and protect themselves, and feel more confident and powerful. Furthermore, it gives people a feeling of virtue and being right despite others' opposition, making them more willing to speak out and challenge people.

Anger acts as a signal alerting people to the fact that something is wrong and leading them to change frustrating and unproductive circumstances. It disrupts ongoing behavior by making people agitated. They want to correct the perceived injustice and counter the aggression. Expressing anger gets the attention of others and motivates them to deal with the conflict.

### Skills for Managing Anger

For an organization to accept and value anger is an important first step. But anger is often suppressed because people do not have confidence that they can deal with it openly. Managing anger is challenging and requires considerable competence.

Other people do not make us angry. Our conclusions that their actions were frustrating, intentional, and illegitimate do. By changing our thinking, we can change our emotions. Research indicates that we also have choices about how we express our anger. Indeed, people usually find it easier to control what they do than what they think (Averill, 1982). People are by no means programmed to deal with anger in one way; they have many options. They can lash out and punish, take it out on someone else, or gossip to get back. They can also talk to others to regain perspective, ventilate, or try talking to the other person without hostility.

## Special Focus: Coping with an Intolerable Boss

Perhaps the most trying situation employees can find themselves in is to have a boss who is not just unaware or unfriendly, but is mean and competitive. Getting such a boss is bad luck, but at least it is shared. Three-fourths of the highly successful executives in three Fortune 100 companies reported that they had had at least one intolerable boss during their careers (Lombardo & McCall, 1984).

Very few of them openly confronted this intolerable boss and even fewer actually changed bosses or got the organization to demote them. But most were able to cope. They tried to minimize their feelings of anger and their desire for revenge. They accepted the boss as the boss. They gave up feelings that the boss should not act as he did and did not concentrate on the unfairness and injustice of his actions. They downplayed their own frustrations and even thought about the situation as one they could learn from. They tried to understand the boss's pathologies and perspectives. They knew the kind of boss they did not want to be; they learned that they wanted to be patient and respectful.

The executives changed their thinking so they weren't so angry. Then they were able to plan ways to work around their bosses. They avoided situations that triggered the boss's anger and used good moods to advantage. They talked to friends, got plenty of exercise, and used other ways to vent their feelings.

---

### Expressing Anger

Although not every angry feeling should be expressed to the person at whom it is directed, a direct approach has the most potential to initiate a productive conflict. The following is a list of rules to keep in mind when expressing anger (Johnson, 1991; Johnson & Tjosvold, 1989).

- *Check assumptions.* No matter how convinced employees are that another has deliberately interfered with or harmed them, they may be mistaken. People can ask questions and probe.
- *Be specific.* The more specific the angry person can be, the less threatening their attack is to another's self-esteem and the easier it is to come up with concrete ways to make amends.
- *Be consistent.* Verbal and nonverbal messages should both express anger. Smiling while expressing anger makes the confrontation confusing.
- *Take responsibility for anger.* Persons expressing anger should let the target know that they are angry and the reasoning and steps they took that made them feel unjustly frustrated.
- *Avoid provoking anger.* Expressing anger through unfair, insulting remarks can make the target of the anger angry too. Such situations can quickly deteriorate.
- *Choose statements carefully.* Anger agitates people and they say things they regret later.
- *Avoid self-righteousness.* Anger should be used to get to the heart of the matter and solve problems, not to flout moral superiority.
- *Be sensitive.* People typically underestimate the impact their anger has on others. It is not usually necessary to dramatize one's anger to get people's attention.
- *Make expression cathartic.* Anger is a feeling to get over with, not to hang on to.
- *Express positive feelings.* Showing positive regard for the person toward whom anger is directed can help that person understand that they themselves are not the target.
- *Celebrate joint success.* Be sure to celebrate the mutual achievement of expressing and responding to anger successfully.

## Ventilating Anger

Direct expression of anger toward the person held accountable is not always possible or desirable. It may not be wise or practical to confront an intolerable boss, a new customer, preoccupied colleagues, and stressed employees. Even when direct expression is possible, it is often useful to express it indirectly first so that it is not strong and overpowering. Vigorous activities such as running, swimming, racket sports, and fast walking are useful. Shouting, screaming, crying, throwing things, and punching pillows release energy. People can also find relief by confiding, complaining, and gossiping. When others listen, such talk helps reduce the power of anger.

## Changing Unrealistic Assumptions

A certain amount of anger is natural and inevitable, but some people find themselves frequently angry. They may be tough on colleagues and customers, and on themselves as well. Often these people have unrealistic assumptions that lead them to think about situations in ways that make them very angry. Common troubling assumptions (Ellis, 1987) include, "I am a good person, everyone should like and respect me," "every person who gets angry at me has acted unjustly and unfairly," "every criticism is designed to make me look foolish and weak so I must counterattack," and "God gave me the right to an uninterrupted lunch hour (or chair, traffic lane, or whatever)."

Employees should identify assumptions that lead to excessive anger, dispose of them, and replace them with more reasonable assumptions.

Experience in managing conflict can help in this learning process. As people realize they have drawn faulty conclusions, they become aware of their faulty assumptions. Then they develop more useful assumptions and argue with themselves until they adopt them.

Constructive assumptions include, "although I am a good person, I will do things that will upset and frustrate others," "people who get angry with me want to make our relationship stronger," "criticism and negative feedback can help me become more self-aware and competent, and "it would be nice if I were left in peace for my lunch hour, but these are nuisances I can live with."

## Recovering Frustrated Customers

Customers are inevitably frustrated, inconvenienced, and angered when organizations make errors and fail to deliver as promised. No matter how hard they try, an airline's ground and flight crews may be unable to reach their destination on time if the destination airport is fogged in. The restaurant may prepare and present the food well, but the customer may simply not like the taste. Even a well-trained frontline employee may, at times, misunderstand a customer's request.

Typically, these service mistakes are best handled by the organization's assuming responsibility and restoring service as quickly as possible. The organization wants to reaffirm its cooperative relationship with customers, deal with the problem expeditiously, and minimize the customer's inconvenience.

Unfortunately, many companies are unprepared to deal with errors and customer frustration. More than half of all efforts to respond to customer complaints have been found to reinforce the customer's negative reactions (Hart, Heskett, & Sasser, 1990). Frontline employees will deny that it is their fault or blame the computer. They will smile and tell the customer to see the supervisor.

However, not responding to customer frustration can have a devastating impact on the business. John Barrier used his bank's parking lot to do business across the street but was told that he had to pay for parking because he had not transacted any business. After cashing a check, he was still refused the parking fee waiver because he had not made a deposit. Though he tried explaining the situation to the branch manager, it was to no avail. Now angry, he paid for his parking, drove to his branch, and explained the incident to his usual banker. He demanded a call by the end of the day. When the call did not come, he withdrew $1 million from his account, and the story hit the evening news. The bank managers hastily tried to recover.

Managers and employees should have a full appreciation of the costs of service breakdowns. Typically, the company calculates the costs of responding to a complaint and making a replacement. But customers almost always pay a price, too, and they don't often forget. They may be stranded, waste time, and miss meetings. With such aggravations, the customer thinks of taking his or her business elsewhere. And losing customers is expensive.

Responding to the customer's frustration and mending the service breakdown can restore confidence and loyalty. A U.S. Office of Consumer Affairs study found that of households with service problems costing more than $100, 54 percent would maintain brand loyalty if their problems were resolved, but only 19 percent would if they were unhappy with the resolution. Surveys have also showed that people who have had a problem dealt with satisfactorily have more brand loyalty than people who have never had a problem or had one and did not complain (Zemke & Schaaf, 1989).

Some highly successful salespeople see a service breakdown as an opportunity to demonstrate how committed they are to the customer (Kouzes & Posner, 1987). They especially relish service breakdowns that are not their fault. Responding to customer frustration can be challenging for the individual and a revealing "moment of truth" for the organization.

Organizations should, of course, strive to develop systems that "do the right thing the first time." But frontline employees and their managers must recognize that there will be problems and friction, and brainstorm about where these areas would most likely be. Then they need to decide how they can best handle problems that do arise. New services and high staff turnover are common predisposing factors for problems.

The first step to service recovery is knowing the customer's problem (Hart, Heskett, & Sasser, 1990). In addition to providing twenty-four-hour hot lines, customer service suggestion boxes, and questionnaires, organizations can encourage frontline employees to ask customers how they felt about the service and if they had any difficulties. Since many customers are uncomfortable expressing anger and complaining, frontline employees need to listen carefully to discover their concerns. British Airways has video booths at Heathrow Airport in London so that passengers can tape their reactions upon arrival. When employees develop relationships with customers it makes it easier for them to speak their minds and reveal a problem.

Once problems are identified, frontline employees should be empowered and trained to quickly restore service and apologize. They should do whatever they can to reduce the cost to the customer. If appropriate, they can try to make amends with a gesture that shows the organization regrets the inconvenience caused the customer. For example, restaurants give patrons a glass of wine or a free dessert. First Union National Bank in Charlotte, North Carolina, sends roses to badly inconvenienced customers.

Although business lore praises individual service heroes, effective service teams are vital for successful management of customer frustrations and complaints. Through discussion, team members understand the cost of poor service recovery and the value of pleasing a customer. They appreciate that management is committed to high-quality service and recovery. They have negotiated with management the authority and power to react quickly to service errors. They identify where and when mistakes are likely to occur and, in addition to making mistakes less likely, anticipate how they can recover and make amends.

## Coping with Provocations

Customers, at times, get angry and vent that anger on employees. They do not always express their anger appropriately. Other employees may also express their anger in ways that are tough to deal with. To manage provocations, people must combine the skills of expressing their anger directly, venting their feelings, modifying their thinking, changing their assumptions, and recovering service. There are concrete steps for dealing with provocations.

- *Before the provocation, develop realistic expectations.* Employees can remind each other of the pressures and limitations they and their customers experience. People have different but not necessarily inferior ways of expressing themselves. It is not realistic to expect them always to communicate in a polite, calm, reasonable way. Nor does it make sense to get angry just because the other person is.
- *During the provocation, experience the outburst and work to cope with*

*it.* People should not take attacks on the company or its service personally, and should remind themselves that angry statements should not be taken literally. The customer is letting off steam, and as soon as the frustration has been released the problem can be addressed. Employees need not doubt themselves, even if the customer doubts them. They should try to take the long view, and eschew counterattack because that would continue the negative interaction in which everyone loses.

- *After the provocation, celebrate the strength and success of keeping cool and managing the situation.* Employees can share their experiences with each other and remember how they were able to minimize the difficulty and strengthen the relationship. They can give each other suggestions about how to be better prepared to respond to future provocations.

Managing anger is one of the most pressing and difficult challenges for people in organizations. Suppressed anger can lead to debilitating stress, physical illness, and emotional turmoil, while angry outbursts are taken as signs of immaturity and lack of personal control. When confronted by angry persons, people sometimes feel threatened and counter with their own self-righteousness.

But anger, when skillfully managed, can initiate productive conflict and strengthen relationships. Employees need to accept each other's anger as a sign that it's time to reflect on their relationships and take steps to improve them. They must use customers' complaints and angry outbursts to learn about important issues and seize opportunities to demonstrate their desire to keep customers. They can then congratulate each other on their success in managing anger.

Jackie, Kamil, and others at Western Security need to work continuously to help each other refine their abilities and deepen their sensitivities to manage conflict and anger as they collaborate with each other and serve customers. The effort is ongoing, but they will find such learning important, intellectually challenging, and emotionally fulfilling.

*Conclusion*

# Nurturing
# the Customer-Responsive,
# Team-based Organization

*From the standpoint of everyday life . . . there is one thing we do know: that man is here for the sake of other men—above all, for those upon whose smile and well-being our own happiness depends, and also for the countless unknown souls with whose fate we are connected by a bond of sympathy. Many times a day I realize how much of my own outer and inner life is built upon the labors of my fellow men, both living and dead, and how earnestly I must exert myself in order to give in return as much as I have received.*

*—Albert Einstein*

"You're having fun?" Martina asked. She and Andre were getting an update from the Maplewood customer team on their progress.

"Definitely," said Beatrice.

"But not so much fun that I couldn't appreciate an all-expense-paid trip to Hawaii," Russ said with a smile. "Wasn't there talk about rich rewards when we began our customer service program?"

"I remember that," Kenneth said. "But Russ and I aren't just thinking of ourselves, of course. We want everyone to go as a team."

"Hawaii has mountains to climb, jungles to survive. . . . The team-building possibilities are endless," said Russ.

**153**

"We promise we wouldn't let trifling extrinsic rewards like a trip to Hawaii get in the way of experiencing the more real, personal pleasures of quality service," said Beatrice.

"I'm glad you brought this up," Martina began, in mock seriousness. "As members of the steering committee, Andre and I see it is as our responsibility to keep the lines of communication open." Her face took on an even more exaggerated expression. "We did talk a lot about a journey, but we were being figurative. We meant a collective movement from the muddling status quo to a place of higher customer service where we have never been before."

"Let me see if I can step in your shoes and really understand you, Martina," said Beatrice with the same exaggerated sobriety. "Does this mean, no Hawaii?"

"You got it," Martina said.

"But the good news is that the journey continues," Andre said.

The Maplewood team members took special pleasure in teasing each other. They were making progress in serving customers and they were building strong relationships within the bank. Maplewood was coming to be considered an important part of the larger corporate effort. They had laid the groundwork, and, while they knew well that this was a beginning, they looked forward to the work ahead.

"This journey, as you put it . . . ," Kenneth began in a thoughtful tone. "It's not a very straight one, at least the way I see us going. We're getting closer to our goal, but it doesn't seem like we'll ever actually arrive."

"Take the 'pull organization,'" Russ said. "Our task force is working hard, even struggling, to figure out how we can implement it effectively. It's not easy."

"There's still lots of things to try, though," said Beatrice. "One of our employees heard that some companies use 'mystery shoppers.' They suggested that we try it."

"What's a 'mystery shopper'?" Andre asked.

"They act like customers but they are hired by the company to rate the service they receive," Beatrice explained. "Companies use the information they get to give feedback and hand out rewards."

"And punishments, too, I assume," said Andre.

"Sure," Beatrice said.

"I can see where that keeps people on their toes; it could be a good incentive," Martina said.

"We thought that it could give us good feedback, too," Russ said. "We could keep track of how the branch is doing."

"But there's a downside to this as well," said Beatrice. "I don't like the idea that we would be checking up on our employees as if we don't trust them, as if they're not motivated."

"It could backfire," Martina agreed.

"Well, another simple suggestion is to ask our customers their preferences in how they want to be served," Russ said. "In addition to finding out what services they want, it's been proposed that we find out how much they want to discuss their general financial situation with us, how much they want to get to know the people in the bank, and so forth. We could get a better understanding of their wants and needs."

"It's a thought. I can see possibilities," said Andre.

"And pitfalls, too," Russ said. "Customers might be embarrassed or confused by poorly worded questions. A good team relationship would help customers be more open with us."

"We were also exploring the idea of breaking the branch down into smaller teams. Each team would have its own customers that it could focus on and take care of," Beatrice said.

"It could help us get closer to our customers and make our services more personal," observed Andre.

"But we are concerned that these teams might undermine the branch's unity," Kenneth said.

"So you see there is no straight road," Beatrice said.

"I guess these ideas have to be discussed, torn apart, and modified," Martina said.

"The truth is not black or white," said Andre.

"But it's not necessarily gray either," Beatrice said. "The best solutions are seldom exactly in the middle."

"And we have to put our solutions to the test by actually trying them out," Russ said. "We have to tinker and experiment and find ways to implement them properly."

"Teamwork needs to guide our experimentation," Martina said. "We need to discuss how to implement changes as a team; the changes should strengthen our commitment to working together to serve customers."

"Here's where my branch and the others need to help," Sandy said. "It's not good that Maplewood does all the experimenting. We run the risk of customers getting annoyed and nervous. They'll ask themselves, '*Now* what are these people doing?' And we don't want them to ask that question."

"That's a good point," Russ said. "I think most customers like to see us trying out new ideas, up to a point. But no matter how much we try to anticipate the problems of implementing an idea, there's going to be snafus and customers will be inconvenienced. We shouldn't use that as an excuse for maintaining the status quo, but we don't want customers to think they're guinea pigs."

People from the other branches agreed that having all the branches experiment lowered the risks for each and would involve more people. They discussed how much they had learned about customer service and teamwork by observing Maplewood; they wanted to reciprocate by sharing the results of their efforts.

"Perhaps the journey is not that crooked," Martina said. "We know where we want to go, and we also know that the whole basis for getting there is working together inside each branch and between the branches."

"We have a direction in our shared vision and our team relationships," Russ summarized. "But we must be creative in how we improve our service."

After meeting with Martina, Andre, Edmund, and Mike, Catherine discussed the steering committee's views on the progress at Maplewood and elsewhere. Her report brought a warm sense of accomplishment to the executive team.

"I'm going to thank the steering committee and the Maplewood team personally," Mark said. "I'm delighted with their work. But we should also be proud. I like it that we can congratulate all of us, the whole team."

"Sometimes it's hard to think that we've done something just by helping others contribute," said Norman.

"We're use to thinking that we must complete a concrete task to get any credit," Peter said.

"It's interesting hearing how they are experimenting with different ideas," Steve said. "They're in a good position to experiment."

"We need to experiment too," Catherine said. "The new products team is getting ready to propose that we offer a broker service at some of the branches. That should provoke an interesting discussion."

"I've got an idea that we may want to try," Norman said. "The essence of the idea is for us to help our commercial customers appreciate the value of customer service and teamwork. We'd be like a living laboratory. In addition to getting financial resources, they could see teamwork and customer service in action, valuable lessons indeed."

"I'd like to explore that idea more," Peter said. "It's different than what I think of banking, but it may be worth a look."

"In a way though, Norman's idea is part of the traditional mandate of banks," Mark said. "We're supposed to help incubate new businesses and develop the local economy. Certainly knowing how to get people to work together to serve customers is required in today's marketplace."

"Norman's idea also fits in with our efforts to be seen as a more vital, active part of the community," said Steve.

"Like the steering committee and branch customer team, we have some experimenting and testing to do," Peter said.

"I think we should consider this idea more, but if I can bring us back to the steering committee and branch team. I think they'd like getting a personal pat on the back," Catherine said.

"Maybe we could have lunch with them; we could get to know each other better too," Mark said.

"Why is it that when we think of getting together, we think of food?" Norman said.

"It may be that we're always hungry," Steve said. "But I like to think that eating together shows we're friends, we're 'family.'"

"The team organization model should add 'eating to-gether' as a way to foster unity," said Peter with a laugh.

"So lunch with the steering committee and customer team is a good idea?" Mark asked. "Let's do it then. I'm glad we can do something direct and concrete to show our gratitude."

"Sounds great," Catherine said. "I heard they were joking about getting a free trip to Hawaii."

"Tell them we don't have customers there to serve, and they would be absolutely bored," Peter quipped, deadpan. "I went there in search of customers and came up empty-handed."

"Bad luck!" Norman laughed.

"I don't believe that our efforts at customer service have shown up dramatically on the bottom line, have they, Catherine?" Mark asked.

"I can't see it in the numbers," said Catherine.

"But if and when it does, I certainly think we should distribute the gains," Mark said. "I'd enjoy handing out money to everyone, even me!"

"The steering committee is considering the idea of a company-wide bonus," Catherine said.

"With the local economy hurting, it may be some time before we have enough profits for a bonus," said Peter.

"We can't judge our success simply by how much money we make in the next quarter," Mark said. "There's too many factors that affect the bottom line that have little to do with how well we're doing. We need the discipline to take the long-term view."

"Banks have gotten in big trouble because they were making lots of money," Peter said. "A friend was telling me about how his bank thought the good times would keep rolling, but when the area's economy took a nosedive, and people stopped moving in, the bank had to get rid of the plane, the cars, all the trappings of success. But it couldn't get rid of its sloppy habits and eventually went belly-up."

"Think of how banks have tried to cope with increased competition and deregulation," Steve said. "They've lent money overseas, often to corrupt despots, speculated in real estate and foreign currency, gotten into stock trading, sponsored mergers and acquisitions. These were all thought to be the next pile of gold, at least the next life boat. Some banks have had to pay big for painful lessons."

"It's stories like these that make me glad we are focused on the basics of quality customer service, of giving real value to our long-term customers," Mark said. "It will keep us sane and profitable."

"And it's fun, too," said Norman.

"Even if we don't make lots of money, we can have fun," Catherine said.

### Linking Together

Mark, Catherine, and their colleagues at Western Security were involving everyone in the organization in delivering value to customers. Serving customers is not something that frontline employees do alone. It is not enough that the president wax eloquent talking about it at dinner meetings. Improving customer service requires collective effort. Every person and every job is valuable and can contribute to creating an organization that deserves the support, money, and gratitude of its customers.

Encounters with customers provide myriad opportunities for a company to succeed or fail. Jan Carlzon, CEO and chairman of Scandinavian Airlines System, wrote that, in every meeting between employee and customer, "the future of the company [hangs] in the balance. I called it the moment of truth; this may not have been wholly original, but it struck me with the force of a revelation" (Gronroos, 1990, p. xv). Fortunately, an organization can get prepared for these tests. Teamwork is the foundation that empowers service providers to reach out, solve problems, and deliver value.

Customer service unites people within a society as well as within an organization. We depend, whether we want to or not, on farmers, physicians, teachers, manufacturers, insurers, and many, many other people and organizations. Even supposedly independent entrepreneurs spend much of their time networking with suppliers, marketing agents, banks, and government regulators (Dollinger, 1985; Tjosvold & Weicker, in press). When a society's organizations develop strong, cooperative interdependence and serve each other, its people flourish. When a society's organizations do not cooperate to serve, people are hit with a triple blow: they are angry that they are not served, frustrated because they cannot serve, and stressed by being pitted against each other.

## Creating Teamwork for Customers

Teamwork is needed to serve customers, but teamwork is also needed to create teamwork. Managers and employees must study, critique, and apply the team organization model together. They learn to work as a team by developing their team. The method reinforces the message. The team organization model suggests how to take vital steps toward realizing the human mission of serving customers.

*Envision Teamwork for Customers*

How can people see the value of working as a team to serve customers and each other? How can its value be demonstrated and skepticism be dealt with directly?

Managers and employees can brainstorm about the imperative to serve customers, learn about the team organization model, and gain a sense of its power and usefulness. Reading books and articles, getting involved in discussions about teamwork and customer service, attending seminars and presentations, and talking to people already experimenting with teamwork to serve customers can help them explore issues further. They should also debate the merits of teamwork and customer service. Perhaps the most convincing evidence, however, comes from putting the model to use.

*Unite Behind the Vision*

How can people see that teamwork for customers pays off for all and unites everyone in a vital, common effort? What experiences can help people identify their priorities and see how they overlap?

Research has documented that, for customers, the payoff of teamwork is real and substantial. The company, its employees, and its customers benefit from improved productivity, innovation, greater challenges and support, and more confidence in the quality of service. We have exposed the myths that a company must choose between being productive or people-oriented, that what is good for management hurts employees, and that what is good for customers frustrates employees.

*Empower Each Other*

How can people understand quality service and the team organization model? What are the confusions that typically get in their way? What are the critical first steps that will clarify what team organization is and show how it can be accomplished?

The organization's leaders must convey their commitment to the vision that people will work as a team to serve customers. Employees should ask questions and figure out what teamwork means to them. Managers and employees together can study the nature of team organization and create workshops, task forces, and other forums to discuss how to apply the principles of team organization to improve customer service.

### Explore How to Serve

How can people work together to forge a team organization? What are the forums most conducive to productive collaboration? What aspects of the structure or of the rewards, training, or other programs can be changed? What aspects cannot be changed and must be lived with?

Service teams and others need to decide how they can best work together to serve customers. Managers and employees should debate the merits of different recommendations for strengthening the team's vision and helping members feel more united, be more empowered, explore issues thoroughly, and reflect for continuous improvement. They can work to achieve a consensus on the company's direction. They can structure job assignments, rewards, and expectations to strengthen unity. They can refine communication and conflict skills to feel empowered.

### Reflect on Teamwork and Customer Service

How can people be encouraged to work together to continuously develop new and better ways of serving customers? What forums and procedures will facilitate feedback and discussion about relationships and conflicts?

Recognizing the need to invest in their groups and organizations, team members must commit themselves to dealing with conflicts directly and openly. They can schedule regular sessions to reflect on how they are working together and assess the quality of the service they are providing. They can form service and learning teams in which they strive for ongoing improvement and celebrate successes.

## Building on the Basics

We are facing new and often disturbing challenges. The power of modern production capabilities and the efficiency of global transportation have heightened competition, threatening many companies and present ways of working. Social agencies are trying to cope with the impact of a weakened nuclear family, increased personal alienation, and the threats of societal disarray. Though some old enemies have become allies, others have started new wars. We often feel like pawns pushed around by turbulent events.

Yet the traditional ideas of commitment to serving people and working together are the keys to helping us meet new challenges. Fancy slogans and hype will not create productive organizations or humane societies. We must review our pledge to work together to serve others.

Investing in relationships and developing organizational teamwork pay off in employee commitment and ongoing innovation. It is through spirited collaboration that an organization can adapt to changes, create new products, and retain and win customers. Working as a team gives people the most enduring competitive advantage.

We need to remind ourselves that serving other people contributes substantially to our own personal well-being. We cannot be successful alone. We cannot develop our individuality, feel confident in ourselves, and pursue our goals by ourselves. Much less can we feel fulfilled by pitting ourselves against each other. Organizations that serve people are the irreplaceable building blocks of a strong society capable of sustaining the psychological and economic health of its people.

Confusion and ambiguity have frustrated us. We have considered serving others to be a demeaning task and have reserved it for entry-level, low-paid employees. We have thought that to be an individual we must depend only on ourselves, that the choice is between the individual and the group. We have equated cooperative teamwork with conformity and preserving the status quo. We have exaggerated the motivational and personal benefits of competition.

Serving people helps us develop our human potential. Cooperative teamwork stimulates spirited controversies, lively support of individuals, and honest discussions of conflicts. Creating this kind of teamwork is possible. Everyone has experienced working with others cooperatively and effectively. Our capacity to work together distinguishes us from other species and helps account for our prominence.

We need to capture traditional teamwork and put it to work meeting untraditional challenges and conditions. Professionals with diverse training and orientations, people from different countries and cultures, and employees in different cities must work together to solve new, complex problems under the pressures of time and budget constraints. Expansive knowledge and persistent work are needed to develop the procedures, skills, and forums of organizational teamwork suitable for today.

You can use the team organization model to create a teamwork that works for you and your customers. You and your colleagues can study together to deepen your common understanding of quality customer service and teamwork and dispel confusions and ambiguities. You can decide to work as a team, reach a consensus on the common framework for joint work, and put spirited teamwork in place. Then you will be prepared to serve your customers and yourselves.

# Appendix

# Guidelines for Action,
# Pitfalls to Avoid

This appendix outlines the action implications of developing teamwork to serve customers. You can use the appendix to review the book's ideas and to stimulate plans for improving customer service in your organization. The guidelines for action and pitfalls to avoid can help you discover important contributors to quality teamwork and customer service. As you experiment with these guidelines and pitfalls, you can rephrase them and create new ones to make them more appropriate for you and your organization.

## Confronting Reality

### Guidelines for Action

- Focus on how serving customers unites the organization.
- Discuss and debate how serving customers well can serve the organization.
- Collect feedback from customers and employees on customer service.
- Consider feedback as an aid for learning and development.
- Celebrate strengths in customer service.
- Plan how to confront weaknesses together.
- Acknowledge the value of all parts of the organization.

*Pitfalls to Avoid*

- Assume the present level of service will continue to be good enough.
- Project an image of such competence that there is no need to learn.
- Dismiss customers and employees who complain as being spoiled.
- Blame individuals and their departments for customer service failures.
- Assign the responsibility for improving customer service to one person or department.
- Believe that telling people to improve service is effective.

## Taking Charge

*Guidelines for Action*

- Recognize that teamwork is the basis for feeling powerful in organizations.
- Discuss common predicaments openly and skillfully.
- Exchange opposing ideas to dig into issues.
- Share the emotional ups and downs of facing problems head-on.
- Empower others so that they can be valuable partners.
- Keep lines of communication and discussion open to help employees feel empowered.
- Acknowledge the need to develop group and conflict skills.

*Pitfalls to Avoid*

- Believe you can be powerful all by yourself.
- Cultivate the image of power.
- Equate power with ordering people around.
- Impose ideas on others.
- Assume empowering means giving others complete autonomy.

## Pull System

### *Guidelines for Action*

- Read articles and discuss the pull system as a team.
- Critique the strengths and weaknesses of pull and push approaches.
- Focus employees on working together to serve customers.
- Combine the best of push and pull organizations.
- Encourage employees to participate in assisting and teaching each other.

### *Pitfalls to Avoid*

- Assume that traditional, individualistic ways of working are effective.
- Discard practices just because they are traditional.
- Equate efficiency with customer service.
- Believe that keeping everyone busy results in effectiveness.
- Assume jobs require specialists who cannot perform other tasks.

## Team Relationships

### *Guidelines for Action*

- Understand that members of a team must feel that they are on the same side in order to work well together, but that this feeling is based on how well team members believe they are being treated.
- Recognize that teamwork is both one thing and many things.
- Discover how the aspects of team organization reinforce each other.
- Continually study the team organization model as you experiment with it.
- Appreciate how effective teamwork requires conflict management.

- Understand how teamwork supports individuality and how individuality contributes to productive teamwork.

## *Pitfalls to Avoid*

- Assume there is no useful theory and research on teamwork.
- Assume we all know about teamwork.
- Confuse cooperation with conflict avoidance.
- Equate competition with conflict.
- Strive to understand everything about teamwork at one setting.
- Assume the choice is between the individual and the group.
- Assume that working as a team requires suppressing the individuals who make up the team.

## Learning Team Organization

### *Guidelines for Action*

- Make a personal, vigorous statement of the leaders' commitment to teamwork and customer service.
- Involve employees in developing ways to help other employees become committed to quality service and teamwork.
- Have employees make explicit the value of serving customers.
- Assign employees parts of the team organization model to teach each other.
- Structure discussion and critique to deepen understanding of quality service and teamwork.
- Assign people who don't know each other to discussion groups and in other ways encourage relationships and communication.
- Work for a shared commitment to becoming a team organization and improving service.
- Use task forces to identify specific ways employees can improve the way they work together to serve customers.

*Pitfalls to Avoid*

- Assume everyone understands why serving customers is important.
- Assume everyone has the same definition of teamwork.
- Keep knowledge about team organization to yourself.
- Equate dissension with disloyalty.
- Try to make specific plans in a large group.
- Make decisions on complex problems without prior consideration by a small problem-solving team.

## Forming Service Teams

*Guidelines for Action*

- Involve frontline employees in forming and strengthening service teams.
- Discuss how teamwork within the company can help employees feel supported and effective and able to serve customers.
- Structure discussion and debate among frontline employees on the nature of quality service and productive teamwork.
- Detail how working on developing team organization will pay off for customers and employees.
- Use questionnaires and interviews to collect feedback on the service team's customers.
- Reflect on feedback from customers.
- Admit that internal teamwork falls short of the ideal and be willing to improve.
- Identify and begin to deal with specific barriers and aids to team success.

*Pitfalls to Avoid*

- Communicate that frontline employees have to improve service by themselves.
- Blame service providers for inadequate service.

- Dismiss feedback from customers as unrealistic grumbling.
- Rest hopes for improved service on individual effort.
- Reward individual employees as if they were independent of others.

## Structuring Service Teams

### Guidelines for Action

- Show how service teams contribute to teamwork for customers.
- Specify how service teams help employees as workers and as people.
- Specify the activities of service teams.
- Work with the teams to help them be effective.
- Learn from mistakes as well as successes.
- Build on the successes of other teams.

### Pitfalls to Avoid

- Let employees fend for themselves.
- Assume that getting employees together means they will support each other.
- Believe only a few people know how to cooperate.

## Working with Customers

### Guidelines for Action

- Invest in customer relationships.
- Communicate a consistent intent to form cooperative relationships with customers, but be flexible in actions.
- Respect customers as people.
- Trust customers so that they trust you.
- Ask for and use the ideas and assistance of customers.
- Be open to influence so customers are open.
- Express genuine warmth and caring for customers.

*Pitfalls to Avoid*

- Believe that employees can establish relationships by themselves.
- Search for one right plan of action good for all situations and customers.
- Prove employees have power and are always right.
- Assume customers are always right and employees always wrong.
- Keep an interpersonal distance from customers.

## Managing Conflict

*Guidelines for Action*

- Create expectations that conflict will occur and can be useful.
- Confront problems and communicate feelings openly.
- Define problems together.
- Understand the costs of resisting and the benefits of resolving the conflict.
- Focus on working together to manage the conflict for mutual benefit.
- Elaborate positions and ideas and list facts, information, and theories that support them.
- Challenge opposing ideas and positions and ask for clarification.
- Reaffirm your confidence in those who are different and show respect and acceptance of others as people.
- Identify strengths in opposing arguments.
- Use approaches that you want others to use.
- Search for new information and integrate new reasoning.
- Create a solution responsive to all points of view.
- Reach an agreement.
- Reaffirm the agreement by implementing it.
- Evaluate the solution and look for ways to improve it.
- Celebrate successfully managing the conflict.

*Pitfalls to Avoid*

- Use one strategy for all circumstances.
- Believe you do not have time to address conflict.
- Assume your position is superior.
- Ignore others' views and needs.
- Prove your ideas are "right" and must be accepted.
- Assume others' goals oppose yours and it's "us versus them."
- Pretend to listen.
- Blame others.
- Interpret opposition to your ideas as a personal attack.
- Refuse to admit weaknesses in your position.

## Managing Anger

*Guidelines for Action*

- Recognize when you are angry.
- Decide how to express it.
- Appreciate that customers typically do not expect to be targets of expressed anger.
- Develop the skills to express anger, ventilate, and change assumptions.
- Form strong relationships that allow direct discussions of anger and conflict.
- Focus on the problem at hand.
- Congratulate yourself when you express anger and respond to it well.
- Recognize that it will take practice for your team to make anger a positive influence.

*Pitfalls to Avoid*

- Let others push your button.
- Blame yourself for feeling angry.
- Blame others.
- Expect others to be perfect.
- Expect yourself to be perfect.

- Take every disagreement as an attack on your competence.
- Be self-righteous.
- Express your anger through sarcasm, slow service, and other indirect methods.
- Use insults to express your strong feelings.
- Wait in ambush for others.
- Assume that because a customer or co-worker is angry with you, you should be angry with them.

# REFERENCES

Albrecht, K., & Zemke, R. (1985). *Service America!* Homewood, Ill.: Dow Jones–Irwin.

Argyris, C. (1970). *Intervention theory and method: A behavioral science view.* Reading, Mass.: Addison-Wesley.

Argyris, C. (1991, May–June). Teaching smart people how to learn. *Harvard Business Review,* pp. 99–109.

Argyris, C., & Schön, D. (1978). *Organizational learning.* Reading, Mass.: Addison-Wesley.

Averill, J. R. (1982). *Anger and aggression: An essay on emotion.* New York: Springer-Verlag.

Barrett, J. (1986). Why major account selling works. *Industrial Marketing Management, 15,* 63–73.

Bertrand, K. (1987, November). National account marketing: Cover story. *Business Marketing,* pp. 43–52.

Bowen, D. E., Chase, R. B., & Cummings, T. G. (1990). *Service management effectiveness.* San Francisco: Jossey-Bass.

Bowen, D. E., & Lawler, E. E., III. (1992, Spring). The empowerment of service workers: What, why, how, and when. *Sloan Management Review,* pp. 31–39.

Brown, S. W., Gummesson, E., Edvardsson, B., & Gustavsson, B. (1991). *Service quality: Multidisciplinary and multinational perspectives.* New York: Lexington Books.

Buzzell, R. D., & Gale, B. T. (1987). *The PIMS principles: Linking strategy to performance.* New York: Free Press.

Chase, R. B., & Bowen, D. E. (1991). Service quality and the service delivery system: A diagnostic framework. In S. W. Brown, E. Gummesson, B. Edvardsson, & B. Gustavsson (Eds.), *Service quality: Multidisciplinary and multinational perspectives* (pp. 157–178) New York: Lexington Books.

Chase, R. B., & Garvin, D. A. (1989, July–August). The service factory. *Harvard Business Review,* pp. 61–69.

Coppett, J. I., & Staples, W. A. (1980). A sales mix model for effective industrial selling. *Industrial Marketing Management, 9,* 31–36.

Cosier, R. A., & Schwenk, C. R. (1990). Agreement and thinking alike: Ingredients for poor decisions. *Academy of Management Executive, 4,* 69–74.

Crosby, L. A. (1991). Building and maintaining quality in the service relationship. In S. W. Brown, E. Gummesson, B. Edvardsson, & B. Gustavsson (Eds.), *Service quality: Multidisciplinary and multinational perspectives* (pp. 269–287). New York: Lexington Books.

Crosby, L. A., Evans, K. R., & Cowles, D. (1990). Relationship quality in services selling: An interpersonal influence perspective. *Journal of Marketing, 54,* 68–81.

Cusumano, M. A. (1988). Manufacturing innovation: Lessons from the Japanese auto industry. *Sloan Management Review, 20,* 29–39.

Dale, A., & Wooler, S. (1991). Strategy and organization for service: A process and content model. In S. W. Brown, E. Gummesson, B. Edvardsson, & B. Gustavsson (Eds.), *Service quality: Multidisciplinary and multinational perspectives* (pp. 191–204). New York: Lexington Books.

Deutsch, M. (1973). *The resolution of conflict.* New Haven, Conn.: Yale University Press.

Deutsch, M. (1980). Fifty years of conflict. In L. Festinger (Ed.), *Retrospections on social psychology* (pp. 46–77). New York: Oxford University Press.

Deutsch, M. Sixty years of conflict. (1990). *International Journal of Conflict Management, 1,* 237–263.

Dollinger, M. J. (1985). Environmental contacts and financial performance of the small firm. *Journal of Small Business Management, 23,* 24–30.

Drucker, P. (1974). Management: Tasks, responsibilities and practices. New York: HarperCollins.

Dwyer, F. R., Schurr, P. H., & Oh, S. (1987). Developing buyer-seller relationships. *Journal of Marketing, 51,* 11–27.

Eisenhardt, K. M. (1989). Making fast strategic decisions in high velocity environments. *Academy of Management Journal, 32,* 543–576.

Eisenhardt, K. M., & Bourgeois, L. J., III. (1988). Politics of strategic decision making in high-velocity environments: Toward a midrange theory. *Academy of Management Journal, 31,* 737–770.

Ellis, A. (1987). The impossibility of maintaining consistently good mental health. *American Psychologist, 42,* 365–375.

Farnham, A. (1989, December 4). The trust gap. *Fortune,* pp. 56–78.

Fisher, R., & Ury, W. (1981). *Getting to yes.* New York: HarperCollins.

Fitzsimmons, J. A. (1990). Making continual improvement a competitive advantage for service firms. In D. E. Bowen, R. B. Chase, & T. G. Cummings (Eds.), *Service management effectiveness* (pp. 284–295). San Francisco: Jossey-Bass.

Frazier, G. L., Spekman, R. E., & O'Neal, C. R. (1988, October). Just-in-time exchange relationship in industrial markets. *Journal of Marketing, 52,* 52–67.

George, W. R., & Gibson, B. E. (1991). Blueprinting: A tool for managing quality in services. In S. W. Brown, E. Gummesson, B. Edvardsson, & B. Gustavsson (Eds.), *Service quality: Multidisciplinary and multinational perspectives* (pp. 73–91). New York: Lexington Books.

Gronroos, C. (1990). *Service management and marketing: Managing the moments of truth in service competition.* New York: Lexington Books.

Grzywinski, R. (1991, May–June). The new old-fashioned banking. *Harvard Business Review,* pp. 87–98.

Hart, C. W. L., Heskett, J. L., & Sasser, W. E., Jr. (1990, July–August). The profitable art of service recovery. *Harvard Business Review,* pp. 148–156.

Harvey-Jones, J. (1989). *Making it happen: Reflections on leadership*. Glasgow: Fontana/Collins.

Heide, J., & John, G. (1992). Do norms matter in marketing relationships? *Journal of Marketing, 56*, 32–44.

Heskett, J. L. (1986). *Managing in the service economy*. Cambridge, Mass.: Harvard Business School Press.

Heskett, J. L. (1990). Rethinking strategy for service management. In D. E. Bowen, R. B. Chase, & T. G. Cummings (Eds.), *Service management effectiveness* (pp. 17–40). San Francisco: Jossey-Bass.

Hundley, J. (1987). J. C. Penney relies on people power. In Y. K. Shetty and V. M. Buehler (Eds.), *Quality, productivity, and innovation: Strategies for gaining competitive advantage* (pp. 81–101). New York: Elsevier.

Jackson, B. B. (1985). *Winning and keeping industrial customers*. New York: Lexington Books.

Janz, T., & Tjosvold, D. (1985). Costing effective vs. ineffective work relationships: A method and first look. *Canadian Journal of Administrative Sciences, 2*, 43–51.

Johnson, D. W. (1991). *Reaching out: Interpersonal skills and self-actualization*. Englewood Cliffs, N.J.: Prentice-Hall.

Johnson, D. W., & Johnson, R. T. (1987). *Creative conflict*. Edina, Minn.: Interaction.

Johnson, D. W., & Johnson, R. T. (1989a). *Cooperation and competition: Theory and research*. Edina, Minn.: Interaction.

Johnson, D. W., & Johnson, R. T. (1989b). *Leading the cooperative school*. Edina, Minn.: Interaction.

Johnson, D. W., Johnson, R. T., & Maruyama, G. (1983). Interdependence and interpersonal attraction among heterogeneous and homogeneous individuals: A theoretical formulation and a meta-analysis of the research. *Review of Educational Research, 53*, 5–54.

Johnson, D. W., Johnson, R. T., Smith, K., & Tjosvold, D. (1990). Pro, con, and synthesis: Training managers to engage in constructive controversy. In B. Sheppard, M. Bazerman, & R. Lewicki (Eds.), *Research in negotiations in organization* (Vol. 2, pp. 139–174). Greenwich, Conn.: JAI Press.

Johnson, D. W., Maruyama, G., Johnson, R. T., Nelson, D., & Skon, S. (1981). Effects of cooperative, competitive, and individualistic goal structures on achievement: A meta-analysis. *Psychological Bulletin, 89,* 47–62.

Johnson, D. W., & Tjosvold, D. (1989). Managing stress and anger in conflict. In D. Tjosvold & D. W. Johnson (Eds.), *Productive conflict management: Implications for organizations* (pp. 193–215). Minneapolis, MN: Team Media.

Jusela, G. E., Chairman, P., Ball, R. A., Tyson, C. E., & Dannermiller, K. D. (1987). Work innovations at Ford Motor. In Y. K. Shetty & V. M. Buehler (Eds.), *Quality, productivity, and innovation: Strategies for gaining competitive advantage* (pp. 123–145). New York: Elsevier.

Kanter, R. M. (1979, July–August). Power failure in management circuits. *Harvard Business Review,* pp. 65–75.

Kirkpatrick, D. (1990, February 12). Environmentalism: The new crusade. *Fortune,* pp. 24–30.

Kouzes, J. M., & Posner, B. Z. (1987). *The leadership challenge: How to get extraordinary things done in organizations.* San Francisco: Jossey-Bass.

Krantz, K. T. (1989, September–October). How Velcro got hooked on quality. *Harvard Business Review,* pp. 34–39.

Lawton, J. A. (1987). In Y. K. Shetty and V. M. Buehler, *Quality, productivity, and innovation: Strategies for gaining competitive advantage* (p. 254). New York: Elsevier.

Lewin, K. (1951). *Field theory in social science.* New York: Harper-Collins.

Lombardo, M. M., & McCall, M. W., Jr. (1984). *Coping with an intolerable boss.* Greensboro, NC: Center for Creative Leadership.

Maier, N. R. F. (1970). *Problem-solving and creativity in individuals and groups.* Pacific Grove, CA: Brooks/Cole.

Michaels, R. E., & Day, R. L. (1985). Measuring customer orientation of salespeople: A replication with industrial buyers. *Journal of Marketing Research, 22,* 443–446.

Normann, R. (1984). *Service management.* New York: Wiley.

Nultry, P. (1990, May 21). The soul of an old machine. *Fortune,* pp. 49–54.

Parasuraman, A., Berry, L. L., & Zeithaml, V. A. (1991). Understanding, measuring, and improving service quality: Findings from a multiphase research program. In S. W. Brown, E. Gummesson, B. Edvardsson, & B. Gustavsson (Eds.),

*Service quality: Multidisciplinary and multinational perspectives* (pp. 235–268). New York: Lexington Books.

Perdue, B. C., Day, R. L., & Michaels, R. E. (1986). Negotiation styles of industrial buyers. *Industrial Marketing Management, 15,* 171–176.

Pfeffer, J. (1981). Power in organizations. Boston: Pittman.

Pruitt, D. (1981). *Negotiation behavior.* San Diego, Calif.: Academic Press.

Quinn, J. B., & Paquette, P. C. (1990). Service technologies: Key facts in manufacturing strategy. In D. E. Bowen, R. B. Chase, T. G. Cummings, & Associates, *Service management effectiveness* (pp. 64–94). San Francisco: Jossey-Bass.

Saxe, R., & Weitz, B. A. (1982). The SOCO scale: A measure of the customer orientation of salespeople. *Journal of Marketing Research, 19,* 343–351.

Schneider, B., & Bowen, D. E. (1985). Employee and customer perceptions of service in banks: A replication and extension. *Journal of Applied Psychology, 70,* 423–433.

Seligman, M. (1988, October 22). Boomer blues. *Psychology Today,* pp. 50–55.

Sellers, P. (1990, June 4). What customers really want. *Fortune,* pp. 62–68.

Shostack, G. L. (1984, January–February). Designing services that deliver. *Harvard Business Review,* pp. 133–139.

Soldow, G. F., & Thomas, G. P. (1984). Relational communication: Form versus content in the sales interaction. *Journal of Marketing, 48,* 84–93.

Spekman, R. E., & Johnston, W. J. (1986). Relationship management: Managing the selling and the buying interface. *Journal of Business Research, 14,* 514–553.

Straatman, M. (1990). Quoted in J. M. Kouzes & B. Z. Posner, *The leadership challenge: How to get extraordinary things done in organizations* (pp. 122–123). San Francisco: Jossey-Bass.

Swartz, T. A., & Brown, S. W. (1991). An evolution of research on professional service quality. In S. W. Brown, E. Gummesson, B. Edvardsson, & B. Gustavsson (Eds.), *Service quality: Multidisciplinary and multinational perspectives* (pp. 237–249). New York: Lexington Books.

Tjosvold, D. (1981). Unequal power relationships within a cooperative or competitive context. *Journal of Applied Social Psychology, 11,* 137–150.

Tjosvold, D. (1984a). Cooperation theory and organizations. *Human Relations, 37,* 743–767.

Tjosvold, D. (1984b). Effects of crisis orientation on managers' approach to controversy in decision making. *Academy of Management Journal, 27,* 130–138.

Tjosvold, D. (1985a). Implications of controversy research for management. *Journal of Management, 11,* 21–37.

Tjosvold, D. (1985b). Power and social context in superior-subordinate interaction. *Organizational Behavior and Human Decision Processes, 35,* 281–293.

Tjosvold, D. (1985c). The effects of attribution and social context on superiors' influence and interaction with low performing subordinates. *Personnel Psychology, 38,* 361–376.

Tjosvold, D. (1986). *Working together to get things done: Managing for organizational productivity.* Lexington, Mass.: Heath.

Tjosvold, D. (1987). Participation: A close look at its dynamics. *Journal of Management, 13,* 739–750.

Tjosvold, D. (1988). Cooperative and competitive interdependence: Collaboration between departments to serve customers. *Group & Organization Studies, 13,* 274–289.

Tjosvold, D. (1989a). Interdependence and conflict management in organizations. In M. A. Rahim (Ed.), *Managing conflict: An interdisciplinary approach* (pp. 41–50). New York: Praeger.

Tjosvold, D. (1989b). *Managing conflict: The key to making your organization work.* Minneapolis, Minn.: Team Media.

Tjosvold, D. (1990). Power in cooperative and competitive organizational contexts. *Journal of Social Psychology, 130,* 249–258.

Tjosvold, D. (1991a). *The conflict-positive organization: Stimulate diversity and create unity.* Reading, Mass.: Addison-Wesley.

Tjosvold, D. (1991b). *Team organization: An enduring competitive advantage.* New York: Wiley.

Tjosvold, D. (1991c). Rights and responsibilities of dissent: Cooperative conflict. *Employee Rights and Responsibilities Journal, 4,* 13–23.

Tjosvold, D. (in press). *Learning to manage conflict: Getting people to work together productively.* New York: Lexington Books.

Tjosvold, D., Andrews, I. R., & Struthers, J. T. (1991). Power and interdependence in work groups: Views of managers and employees. *Group & Organization Studies, 16,* 285–299.

Tjosvold, D., Andrews, I. R., & Struthers, J. T. (in press). Leadership influence: Goal interdependence and power. *Journal of Social Psychology.*

Tjosvold, D., Dann, V., & Wong, C. L. (1992). Managing conflict between departments to serve customers. *Human Relations, 45,* 1–20.

Tjosvold, D., Meredith, L., & Weldwood, R. M. (1991). *Implementing relationship marketing: A goal interdependence approach.* Unpublished manuscript, Simon Fraser University, Burnaby, British Columbia.

Tjosvold, D., & Tjosvold, M. M. (1991). *Leading the team organization: How to create an enduring competitive advantage.* New York: Lexington Books.

Tjosvold, D., Tjosvold, M. M., & Tjosvold, J. (1991). *Love & Anger: Managing family conflict.* Minneapolis, Minn.: Team Media.

Tjosvold, D., & Weicker, D. (in press). Cooperative and competitive networking by entrepreneurs: A critical incident study. *Journal of Small Business Management.*

Tjosvold, D., & Wong, C. (1990). *Marketing high technology: A study of goal interdependence and conflict.* Unpublished manuscript, Simon Fraser University, Burnaby, British Columbia.

Tjosvold, D., & Wong, C. (1991, June). *Goal interdependence approach to conflict in the buyer-seller relationship.* Paper presented at the meeting of the International Association for Conflict Management, Amsterdam, The Netherlands.

Tjosvold, D., & Wong, C. L. (1992, June). *Cooperative conflict and coordination to market technology.* Paper presented at the International Association of Conflict Management conference, Minneapolis, Minn.

Webber, A. M. (1991, May–June). Crime and management: An interview with New York City Police Commissioner Lee P. Brown. *Harvard Business Review,* pp. 111–126.

Weitz, B. A., Sujan, H., & Sujan, M. (1986). Knowledge, motivation, and adaptive behavior: A framework for improving selling effectiveness. *Journal of Marketing, 50,* 174–191.

Weitzel, W., & Jonsson, E. (1991). Reversing the downward spiral: lessons from W. T. Grant and Sears Roebuck. *Academy of Management Executive, 5,* 7–21.

Williams, A. J., & Seminerio, J. (1985). What buyers like from salesmen. *Industrial Marketing Management, 14,* 75–78.

Wong, C. L., & Tjosvold, D. (in press). Goal interdependence and service quality in services marketing. *Psychology & Marketing Journal.*

Zemke, R., & Schaaf, D. (1989). *The service edge: 101 companies that profit from customer care.* New York: New American Library.

# INDEX

## A

Accountability, of team members, 75, 76, 77. *See also* Punishments; Rewards

Advertising: as communication, 111; overpromising in, 5

Agreement, in conflict management, 134-135, 136, 171

Albrecht, K., 11

Allen-Bradley, 16

Anderson, R., 32

Andrews, I. R., 48

Anger: and assumptions, 148; causes of, 143-144; and customer frustration, 149-151; and customer provocation, 151-152; expression of, 141-142, 146-147; management of, 145-148, 152, 172-173; nonavoidance of, 142-143, 152; positive side of, 144-145; stereotypes about, 142-143; ventilation of, 147-148. *See also* Conflict management; Customers; Emotions

Argyris, C., 30, 80

Assessment: of customer service, 20-29, 31, 35; guidelines for, 165; of organizational vision, 72, 73; pitfalls of, 166; of teamwork, 79-81

Assumptions, changing of, 148

Assurance, customer expectation of, 4

Auto repair business, customer service in, 112

Autonomy, in teamwork, 50, 51, 53-54, 166. *See also* Empowerment; Teamwork

Averill, J. R., 143, 144, 145

Avoidance, of conflict, 130-131. *See also* Conflict management; Defensiveness

## B

Baldwin, J., 20

Ball, R. A., 30

Banking industry, customer service in, 113-116, 149. *See also* Western Security Bank

Barrett, J., 9, 103

Barrier, J., 149

Benefits, as customer expectation, 4

Berry, L. L., 4

Bertrand, K., 9, 103

Bhopal refinery accident, 4

Blueprinting, for managing service quality, 103

Bonus systems. *See* Rewards

Bosses. *See* Superiors

Bottom line, effect of competition on, 9

Bottom-line management, 39

Bourgeois, L. J., III, 34, 131

Bowen, D. E., 14, 29, 116

British Airways, 150

Brown, L. P., 48, 49

Brown, S. W., 128

Budget, and customer service, 39

Burger King, 111–112

Business lore, and heroic service, 3

## C

Car rental business, customer service in, 93–95

Carlzon, J., 160

Case studies: Banking with Chicago's South Side, 113–116; Empowering New York City Police, 48–50; Innovation and Coordination at Interrent, 93–95; Milacron Pulls Ahead of the Competition, 62–63; W. T. Grant's Downward Spiral, 31–33. *See also* Western Security Bank

Celebration, of team accomplishments, 73. *See also* Rewards

Chairman, P., 30

Chase, R. B., 14, 15, 29

Chinese proverb, 76, 85

Chlorofluorocarbons (CFCs), 137. *See also* Environmentalism

Clark, R., 137

Commitment. *See* Vision

Communication: and customer service, 11; with customers, 109, 111, 116; within organization, 47, 104, 166, 168. *See also* Conflict management; Customer service; Customer service team; Discussion; Teamwork

Competition, internal, 39–42, 74; dangers of, 34, 78–79; overcoming of, 42–46. *See also* Competitive workstyle; Divisiveness; Marketplace

Competitive workstyle, 5–6; versus cooperative, 7, 8, 9, 10, 12; coping with, 146. *See also* Competition

Complaints, customer, 129–130; and

innovation, 129–130; responding to, 149–150. *See also* Conflict management; Customers; Customer service; Customer service team

Conflict management: and anger, 144, 145, 148; and conflict avoidance, 130–131; cooperative style of, 129–138; between customers and teams, 123–138; dynamics of, 132–138; guidelines for, 171; and mutual benefit, 131; obstacles to, 133, 134; within organization, 70, 73, 77–79, 80–81, 89, 97–99, 167, 168; pitfalls of, 172; and reaching agreement, 134–135; rewards of, 135–136. *See also* Anger; Discussion; Frustration

Confrontation. *See* Conflict management; Controversy; Discussion

Contracts, for team members, 104

Controversy: and customer service, 131; rewards of, 135–136; within teams, 78–79. *See also* Conflict management; Discussion

Cooperative workstyle, 6. *See also* Conflict management; Teamwork

Coordination, to solve customer problems, 7–9. *See also* Teamwork

Coppett, J. I., 112

Cosier, R. A., 130

Cowles, D., 11

Creative problem solving, 10. *See also* Conflict management; Discussion; Innovation

Credibility, of company, 7, 97–98, 140

Credit, and customer service, 32

Credit card company, customer service in, 112–113

Crime, reduction of, 49–50

Crisis management, 1, 73. *See also* Push organization

Crosby, L. A., 11

Cross-training, for customer service, 88, 101, 110

Cummings, T. G., 14

Customer audit, 24–25

Customer service: assessment of, 20–29, 31, 35, 72; benefits of, 43; to meet competition, 54–55; failure in, 1, 4, 4–5, 149–150, 166; focus on, 21, 159-164; guidelines for, 170; individual versus team approach to, 3-19; motivating employees for, 55-57; pitfalls of, 171. *See also* Customers; Customer service team; Defensiveness; Inferior service; Pull organization; Quality, service

Customer service team: and conflict management, 123-138; development of, 83; expansion of, 156-164; guidelines for, 169, 170; and handling customer frustration, 151; leadership support for, 85-95; and long-term customer relationships, 117-119; pitfalls of, 169-170; and service guarantees, 93-95; structuring of, 96-105; value of, 103-104. *See also* Customer service; Team organization; Teamwork

Customers: conflict with, 128-129, 138; and conflict avoidance, 130, 131; dissatisfaction of, 4-5; 25, 26, 141; expectations of, 4-5; feedback from, 25, 29, 109, 165, 170; listening to, 7-8; and long-term interests, 10, 11-12; loyalty of, 22, 150; provocations by, 151-152; and pull versus push organization, 61; and product focus, 10-11; recovery of, 149-151; retention of, 112; and specialized needs, 11. *See also* Conflict management; Complaints; Customer service; Customers service team; Relational marketing

Cusumano, M. A., 15

**D**

Dale, A., 29
Dann, V., 10
Dannermiller, K. D., 30
Day, R. L., 112, 116, 128
Decision making, within team organization, 77-79. *See also* Autonomy; Team organization
Defensiveness, about customer service failure, 20-28; case study of, 31-33; management of, 29-31

Delivery system. *See* Service delivery system
Deregulation, effect of, 59
Deutsch, M., 128, 131
Devil's advocate, and teamwork, 79
Dialogue. *See* Discussion
Discrepancies: between customer expectation and service, 4-5; between good service and performance, 20-35
Discussion: benefits of, 46-47; and conflict management, 128-129, 132-135; with customers, 126-128, 140; for customer service, 118; and employee empowerment, 76; open, 129-130; within team organizations, 12, 13, 34, 42-43, 44-45, 77. *See also* Conflict management
Diversity, benefits and management of, 77-79. *See also* Conflict management; Discussion; Employees
Divisiveness, within organizations, 22, 25-27, 34, 160; breaking through, 39-46; and conflict avoidance, 131. *See also* Competition; Competitive workstyle; Team organization
Dollinger, M. J., 160
Dow Chemical Company, 4
Du Pont, 136-137
Dumas, A., 74
Dwyer, F. R., 112

**E**

Efficiency: and pull versus push organization, 60; through teamwork, 10
Einstein, A., 153
Eisenhardt, K. M., 34, 131
Electronic equipment manufacturing, 15-16. *See also* Manufacturing
Ellis, A., 148
Emmons, N., 1
Emotions: in company-customer relationship, 10; and customer conflict, 123; about customer feedback, 30, 31; in teamwork, 46, 47, 76, 166. *See also* Anger; Defensiveness; Frustration
Empathy, as customer expectation, 4
Employees: giving autonomy to, 51;

and conflict management, 130, 131, 138; and customer service team, 99–102, 103, 109, 112; and developing team organization, 18, 34–35, 67–68, 70, 168; dissatisfaction of, 25–26, 27; diversity among, 77–79; individuality of, 18, 79, 168; and just-in-time methods, 64, 65; motivating of, 55–59, 72–73; 85–90, 162; observation of, 118, 154–155; in pull versus push organizations, 61; and shared vision, 72–73. *See also* Autonomy; Frontline employees; Managers; Service providers

Empowerment: of customers, 108–109; of frontline employees, 151; guidelines for, 166; pitfalls of, 166; of team members, 75–77; through teamwork, 13, 18, 46–50, 54, 102, 107, 162–163. *See also* Autonomy; Team organization; Teamwork

Engineering companies, and customer service, 8, 9

Entertainment industry, and heroism, 3

Enthusiasm, about customer service, 55–59. *See also* Customer service; Teamwork

Entrepreneurs, as heroes, 3

Environmental groups versus industry, conflict management of, 136–138

Ernst & Young, 111

Ethics. *See* Value statement

Evans, K. R., 11

Exercise, for venting anger, 140, 148

Exxon oil spill, 4, 136

**F**

Factories. *See* Manufacturing; Service factory

Faig, H., 62, 63

"Failpoints," analysis of, 104

Fast food restaurants: and customer service, 111–112; and environmentalism, 137–138

Feelings. *See* Emotions

Finland, service sector in, 14

First Union National Bank, 151

Fisher, R., 135

Fitzsimmons, J. A., 63, 64

Flexibility, in conflict management, 133, 134

Focus groups, 109

Folklore, and heroic service, 3

Ford, 30–31

Fortune 100 companies, 146

Frazier, G. L., 11

Free speech, right to, 79

Frontline employees: and customer expectations, 4; and customer relationships, 112, 116–118, 169; empowerment of, 151; and handling complaints, 149–151; and organizational interdependence, 5, 103; and team organization model, 18. *See also* Customer service team; Employees; Service providers

Frustration: and anger, 143; decision making about, 144; management of, 139–152. *See also* Anger; Conflict management; Customers; Emotions

**G**

Garvin, D. A., 15

General Motors, 10, 77

George, W. R., 103

Gibson, B. E., 103

Gilman, C. P., 39

Gronroos, C., 11, 14, 93, 95, 160

Groups, developing effectiveness in, 70, 74–75. *See also* Team organization; Teamwork

Grzywinski, R., 113

Guarantees, customer service, 93–95

**H**

Harvey-Jones, 14–15

Heide, J., 10

Heroism, in service, 3–4

Heschel, A., 3

Heskett, J. L., 14, 112, 149, 150

Hewlett-Packard, 16

Hierarchy, inversion of, 56–57. *See also* Pull organization

Housing. *See* Residential development

Howell, B., 37
Human nature: and heroism, 3; and service, 163–164
Human relations. *See* Conflict management; Interpersonal relations

**I**

ICI, 14
Identity, team, 75
Image, organizational, 22–23
Impersonality, of service, 1. *See also* Personalism
Incentives. *See* Rewards
Independent workstyle, 5, 74, 167; versus cooperative, 7, 8, 9, 10, 12
Industrial marketing, service teams in, 103
Inferior service: collective responsibility for, 4; and customer expectations, 4–5. *See also* Customer service: Quality, service
Innovation: and conflict management, 134; and customer complaints, 129–130; need for, 41–42; and pull system, 60–65; and shared vision, 73
Interdependence, organizational: benefits of, 6–7; management of, 5–6. *See also* Team organization; Teamwork
Interpersonal skills, development of, 101. *See also* Customer service team
Interrent, 93–95
Inventory, zero versus traditional, 63–64. *See also* Just-in-time

**J**

Jackson, B. B., 9, 112
Janz, T., 9
Japanese companies: competition from, 30, 62, 63; teamwork in, 15
Jigsaw method, 92, 100
Jobs, S., 72
John, G., 10
Johnson, D. W., 6, 7, 11, 92, 112, 118, 130, 132, 147
Johnson, R. T., 6, 7, 92, 118, 130, 132

Johnson, S., 52, 123
Jonsson, E., 31
Jusela, G. E., 30
Just-in-time (JIT), 57; applied to service companies, 63–65. *See also* Pull organization

**K**

Kanter, R. M., 48
Kendrick, J., 32
Kennedy, J. F., 114
Kirkpatrick, D., 136, 138
Kouzes, J. M., 48, 72, 150
Kozak, B., 62
Krantz, K. T., 10

**L**

Land, M., 137
Lawler, E. E., III, 116
Lawton, J. A., 106
Leaders, role of: in encouraging teamwork, 72, 162, 168; in supporting service team, 85–96. *See also* Management
Learning, group, 74–75. *See also* Team organization
Lewin, K., 67, 80, 81
Liaison, between management and task force, 53
Lincoln, A., 83
Lines. *See* Waiting lines
Listening: and anger, 148; in conflict management, 132–133; to customers, 7–8; to team members, 79. *See also* Conflict management; Discussion
Lombardo, M. M., 146
Long-term customer relationships. *See* Relational marketing
Long-term interests, 134. *See also* Relational marketing

**M**

McCall, M. W., Jr., 146
McDonald's, 137–138
Machinery company, pull organization in, 62–63

Maier, N.R.F., 130
Management: and customer expecta-
    tions, 4; and employee empower-
    ment, 76; and teamwork, 34, 52–
    53, 71. *See also* Leaders; Managers
Managers: and conflict avoidance,
    130; and cooperative power, 48;
    and customer expectations, 4; and
    customer feedback, 30–31; and cus-
    tomer service, 7, 8; and developing
    service teams, 86–90, 96–97; in
    pull versus push organizations, 61;
    and teamwork, 37–38, 47, 52–53.
    *See also* Employees; Management
Mandate, organizational, 76. *See also*
    Vision
Manufacturing, teamwork in, 14–17.
    *See also* Just-in-time; Machinery
    company
Marketing. *See* Marketing department;
    Relational marketing; Transac-
    tional marketing
Marketing department, 16: and cus-
    tomer relations, 116; and pull
    versus push organization, 61. *See
    also* Industrial marketing; Sales
    representatives
Marketplace, competition in, 54–55,
    59, 163
Maruyama, G., 7
MasterCare, 112
Mayer, R., 32
MBNA America, 112–113
Meredith, L., 10
Michaels, R. E., 112, 116, 128
Milacron, 62–63
Mission statement, 73. *See also* Vision
Motivation. *See* Customer service; Em-
    ployees
Multi-disciplinary teams, 60. *See also*
    Task force; Steering committee;
    Team organization; Teamwork
Mutual benefit, in problem solving,
    131, 132, 138. *See also* Conflict
    management; Teamwork
"Mystery shoppers," 154–155

### N

Natural Resources Defense Council,
    137

Negotiation, 133, 134–135. *See also*
    Conflict management; Discussion
Nelson, D., 7
New York City Police Department,
    48–50
Nultry, P., 62

### O

Oh, S., 112
O'Neal, C. R., 11
Openness, encouragement of, 79. *See
    also* Conflict management; Con-
    troversy; Discussion
Opinion Research Corporation,
    111–112
Organizational disunity, as cause of
    customer dissatisfaction, 4–5. *See
    also* Divisiveness

### P

Pacific Gas and Electric Company
    (PG&E), 137
Page, T., 30–31
Paine, T., 80
Paper production, and environmental-
    ism, 137
Paquette, P. C., 14
Parasuraman, A., 4
Penney, J. C., 37
Perdue, B. C., 128
Personalism, in customer service, 11,
    108, 111–113. *See also* Relational
    marketing
Personal regard, within teamwork, 79
Pfeffer, J., 48
Plastics, and environmentalism,
    137–138
Policing, community, 48–50
Position, in conflict management,
    132–133
Posner, B. Z., 48, 72, 150
Power, traditional, 47–48, 51, 166. *See
    also* Competition; Empowerment;
    Teamwork
Pride, in product, 6–7
Product, versus service, 14. *See also*
    Manufacturing
Productivity, keeping track of, 74
Pruitt, D., 132

Pull organization, 38, 52–66; case study on, 62–63; and customer relations, 110–111; guidelines for, 167; implications of, 65–66; and just-in-time, 63–65; pitfalls of, 167; and product innovation, 60; compared with push system, 57–58, 61, 65. *See also* Just-in-time

Punishment, for unproductive teamwork, 75, 77. *See also* Rewards

Push organization: outdatedness of, 59–60; compared with pull organization, 57–58, 61, 65. *See also* Pull organization

## Q

Quality, service: determinants of, 29; management of, 103; measurement of, 4. *See also* Inferior service; Customer service; Customer service team

Quality control, 16

Quinn, J. B., 14

## R

Reality, confronting. *See* Defensiveness

Recovery, of service, 149–151

Relational marketing, 10, 11–12; and teamwork, 11–12, 116–117; value of, 111–116

Relationships, in teamwork, 67–81; and managing diversity, 77–79; and promoting unity, 74–75; and shared vision, 72–73. *See also* Team organization; Teamwork

Reliability, as customer expectation, 4, 5

Residential development, investment in, 114–115

Resources, and empowerment, 76

Responsiveness: as customer expectation, 4, 5; and teamwork, 7–8

Rewards, bonus system for, 88, 89, 113, 159; and compensation system, 101; for successful teamwork, 75, 77, 105. *See also* Punishment

Risk taking, and shared vision, 73

## S

Sales representatives: and customer complaints, 150; and relational marketing, 112; and serving customers, 116, 117; and teamwork, 9–10. *See also* Marketing department

Sand, H. A., 94–95

Sasser, W. E., Jr., 112, 149, 150

Saxe, R., 116

Scandinavian Airlines System, 160

Schaaf, D., 129, 150

Schon, D., 30

Schurr, P. H., 112

Schwenk, C. R., 130

Sellers, P., 111, 112, 113

Seminerio, J., 11

Seneca, 72

Service delivery system, analysis of, 103–104. *See also* Customer service; Customer service team; Speed of delivery

Service factory, 15–16, 17

Service providers: in pull versus push organization, 61; and relational marketing, 112, 116; and team organization, 117. *See also* Employees; Frontline employees

Service quality. *See* Quality, service

Service sector, 14, 64

Shostack, G. L., 103

Skills, and empowerment, 76, 77. *See also* Cross-training; Interpersonal skills

Skon, S., 7

Sloan, A., 77–78

Slogans, 33, 67, 93

Smith, C., 113

Smith, K., 130

Socializing, among team members, 75, 140

Soldow, G. F., 11, 112

South Shore Bank, 113–116

Special Focus: Coping with an Intolerable Boss, 146; The Jigsaw Method, 92; Just-In-Time for Service Companies, 63–65; Managing Environmental Conflicts, 136–138; Teamwork in Manufacturing, 14–17

Speed of delivery, 108
Spekman, R. E., 11, 112
Staley, Chrm., 32
Staples, W. A., 112
Status quo, 80
Steering committee, for customer ser-
    vice team, 52–59, 67, 85–86; and
    employee relations, 101–102. *See
    also* Task force
Straatmann, M., 96
Strategic direction. *See* Vision
Stress. *See* Anger; Frustration
Struthers, J. T., 48
Sujan, H., 112
Sujan, M., 112
Superiors, coping with, 146
Support groups, 118
Swartz, T. A., 128
Sweden: service sector in, 14; team-
    work in, 93–95
Synergy, 38, 93

**T**

Taco Bell, 112
Task forces, examples of, 90, 101–102,
    106, 109–110; power of, 4–46, 51;
    within team organizations, 13, 60;
    168. *See also* Steering Committee
Team organization, 12–17; assessment
    of, 79–81; competition in, 97; com-
    ponents of, 71–81; and customer
    relationships, 106–117; decision
    making within, 77–79; dynamics
    of, 13; elements of, 67–81; guide-
    lines for, 168; implementation of,
    91; for internal and external rela-
    tionships, 102–103, 106–110; and
    jigsaw method, 92, 100; in
    manufacturing, 14–17; model of,
    17–19, 38, 69, 70–71, 81, 87–88,
    160; nature of, 12–13; pitfalls of,
    169; promoting cooperation in,
    74–75; in pull versus push organi-
    zation, 61; role of leaders in, 72,
    85–95; and shared vision, 71–73,
    74. *See also* Customer service team;
    Teamwork
Teamwork: and anger, 144–145; bar-
    riers to, 50; benefits of, 6–7, 8–9,
10, 19, 34–35; for coping with cus-
    tomer feedback, 30–31; failure to
    develop, 32; guidelines for, 167;
    and human development, 164; in-
    centives for, 8; and management-
    employee relationships, 67–68,
    99–102; and managing emotions,
    139–152; pitfalls of, 168; power of,
    39–51; promotion of, 74–75; and
    pull organization, 66; research on,
    7–12; spirit of, 1, 42–43; and just-
    in-time, 63–65. *See also* Customer
    service team; Pull organization;
    Team organization
Technology, for customer service, 17,
    65, 89–90, 108–109
Tektronix, 15–16
Telecommunications company, and
    customer service, 8
"Tell and sell" approach, 91
Thomas, G. P., 11, 112
Tjosvold, D., 6, 8, 9, 10, 11, 12, 18,
    32, 46, 47, 48, 71, 78, 81, 89, 92,
    117, 118, 128, 130, 131, 132, 136,
    138, 143, 147, 160
Tjosvold, J., 143
Tjosvold, M. M., 18, 143
Transactional marketing, 10–11
Travel industry, cooperation in, 11–12
Trust: and anger, 142; in customer
    relationships, 107, 108, 117, 170
Twain, M., 121
Tyson, C. E., 30

**U**

U.S. Office of Consumer Affairs, 150
Understanding, in conflict manage-
    ment, 133
United States, service sector in, 14
Unity, within team organization, 71,
    74–75, 80, 161. *See also* Team orga-
    nization; Teamwork; Vision
Ury, W., 135

**V**

Value statement, 75
Variety stores, and customer service,
    31–33

Velcro, 10
Vision, common: with community,
  115; development of, 20–24, 28,
  19, 72–73, 89, 168; and integrated
  approach, 33; and negative feelings, 143; in team organization,
  13–14, 71–73, 74, 91, 161

## W

W. T. Grant, 31–33
Waiting lines, as service defect,
  64
Webber, A. M., 48
Weicker, D., 160
Weitz, B. A., 112, 116
Weitzel, W., 31
Weldwood, R. M., 10
Western Security Bank (fictional case
  study): and building long-term cus-
  tomer relationships, 106–111; and
  customer conflict management,
  123–128; and developing pull orga-
  nization, 52–59; and developing

spirited teamwork, 39–46; and developing team organization, 67–71;
  and encouraging service teams,
  85–90; and evaluating customer
  service, 20–28; and expanding
  team-based customer service,
  153–159; and structuring service
  teams, 96–102
Whitman, W., 139
Williams, A. J., 11
Wong, C. L., 10, 11, 117
Woolard, E., 136
Wooler, S., 29
Workshops, for developing customer
  service team, 86–90, 99–100
Workstyles, 5–6

## Z

Zeithaml, V. A., 4
Zemke, R., 11, 129, 150
Zero inventory. See Inventory
Zero-sum power, 47–48, 51. See also
  Power